Experiential Education in the College Context

Experiential Education in the College Context provides college and university faculty with pedagogical approaches that engage students and support high-impact learning. Organized around four essential categories—active learning, integrated learning, project-based learning, and community-based learning—this resource offers examples from across disciplines to illustrate principles and best practices for designing and implementing experiential curriculum in the college and university setting. Framed by theory, this book provides practical guidance on a range of experiential teaching and learning approaches, including internships, civic engagement, project-based research, service learning, game-based learning, and inquiry learning. At a time when rising tuition, consumer-driven models, and e-learning have challenged the idea of traditional liberal education, this book provides a compelling discussion of the purposes of higher education and the role experiential education plays in sustaining and broadening notions of democratic citizenship.

Jay W. Roberts is Associate Vice President of Academic Affairs and Director of the Center for Integrated Learning at Earlham College, USA.

Experiential Education in the College Context

What it is, How it Works, and Why it Matters

Jay W. Roberts

Routledge
Taylor & Francis Group

NEW YORK AND LONDON

First published 2016
by Routledge
711 Third Avenue, New York, NY 10017

and by Routledge
2 Park Square, Milton Park, Abingdon, Oxon, OX14 4RN

Routledge is an imprint of the Taylor & Francis Group, an informa business

Library of Congress Cataloging in Publication Data
    Roberts, Jay W.
    Experiential education in the college context: what it is, how it works,
    and why it matters/by Jay W. Roberts.
    pages cm
    Includes bibliographical references and index.
    1. College teaching—Methodology. 2. Experiential learning. I. Title.
    LB2331.R53 2016
    378.1'25—dc23
    2015013767

ISBN: 978-1-138-02559-2 (hbk)
ISBN: 978-1-138-02560-8 (pbk)
ISBN: 978-1-315-77499-2 (ebk)

Typeset in Bembo and Bell Gothic
by Florence Production Ltd, Stoodleigh, Devon, UK

MIX
Paper from
responsible sources
FSC
www.fsc.org   FSC® C013056

Printed and bound in Great Britain by
TJ International Ltd, Padstow, Cornwall

To the students, faculty, and staff of Earlham College, where the live encounter carries on at the heart of it all.

Contents

Preface

As I sit in my office on a cold and windy March day and look across campus, I see old Tyler Hall where our admissions office is located and our campus tours begin and end. It is one of our most historic buildings and, when constructed in 1907, Tyler Hall was one of only two Carnegie libraries in Indiana. Looking north from Tyler, I see new construction—"Phase Two" of our science complex at Earlham that will house our Computer Science and Mathematics departments along with state-of-the-art laboratories and classrooms. In contrast with the stately traditional architecture of Tyler Hall, this new complex is the embodiment of "modern" with sleek lines, lots of windows, and a funky design silhouette. It would be too easy, I think, to use these two buildings as archetypes of the academy—one old and outdated and the other new, fresh, and futuristic. But that is not what I take from my gaze out the window. Instead, I see a question hanging above each building in the bright blue sky. To dear old Tyler Hall that question is: How have you managed to survive for all these years despite all the changes that have occurred since your construction in 1907? Tyler Hall has witnessed a great depression, two world wars, the Civil Rights era, the rise of the personal computer, and the Internet. Through it all, despite many changes to its use, it has endured. To the yet-to-be-occupied Phase Two of the science building, the question looks forward rather than behind: What will you see in the next 100 years? Will you even be around in 2115? I wondered, will an academic building like Phase Two have a space and a place in the college of the future?

The physical college or university campus seems a little passé at this particular moment. To some, it is the embodiment of all that is wrong with our system of higher education—it is too expensive, too inflexible, too slow, and too irrelevant for today's global challenges. Many think we should be putting fewer resources into campuses and buildings, and more into online learning platforms. As I will argue in this book, there is nothing inherently wrong with the kind of learning that happens online, and it may in fact be a better educational approach in certain contexts and situations. But an experience I had recently at a conference tells another part of the story.

I was sitting in a large convention center ballroom listening to a big-name keynote speaker talk about the "future of learning in higher education." The audience comprised a fairly diverse mix of teaching faculty, students, and college administrators. The big-named speaker concluded in a flourish extolling the virtues of online learning and the fact that "students these days" wanted more options, more flexibility, and to learn on their own whenever and wherever they wanted. The place-based university was a dinosaur, an outdated relic, that needed to be discarded in favor of this new, better way. As a faculty member, I was skeptical and more than a little bit grumpy about the big-named speaker's argument. Then I looked over to my left and saw a line-up of students waiting to ask questions at the microphone. "Oh great," I thought, "here we go—these students all love her vision and are going to pile on about all the problems of the current system of higher education." But then, something quite remarkable happened. Student after student got up to the microphone and kindly reminded the big-named speaker that, in fact, they *liked* the residential experience of college and that they found it not only to be enjoyable, but *educational*. It turns out they didn't like the idea of learning by themselves. The speaker seemed rather flustered by this turn of events and tried again and again to convince these students that it really was better to learn via videos, online forums, and customized content. The students understood the power of new technology but remained unconvinced. Meanwhile, I sat back rather stunned. I had to admit I, too, was surprised at the passion and commitment students displayed in having a traditional college experience.

However, then it hit me. What the students saw, I think, in this speakers' vision for the future of higher education, was a rather lonely world—a world without sufficient interactive experience. As they stood at the microphone and articulated the value of conversations and experiences in the dorm room, or the cafeteria, or in class with each other, they were expressing a desire for something more than simple efficiency of content delivery. They wanted the chance to connect beyond the computer screen. It reminded me of Maxine Greene in her classic *The Dialectic of Freedom* where she writes of the importance of shared experience.

Making more and more connections in their own experience, reflecting on their shared lives, taking heed of the consequences of the actions they performed, they would become aware of more and more alternatives, more and more experiential possibilities; and this meant an increased likelihood of achieving freedom.

(1988, pp. 42–43)

Freedom, in this sense, is not "doing whatever you want, whenever you want" but in enacting possibility *with others*. Greene goes on to say that "the *person*— that center of choice—develops in his/her fullness to the degree he/she is a member of a live community" (p. 43, emphasis in text). Thus, it is the degree to which experience is *shared* and acted upon collaboratively that makes it, in the end, worthwhile. As Hannah Arendt (1958) noted, "[n]o human life, not even the life of the hermit in nature's wilderness, is possible without a world which directly or indirectly testifies to the presence of other human beings" (p. 22).

I would like to think that the reason that keynote speaker's vision for the future of learning in higher education fell flat was because she misunderstood the importance of the live community in learning—of *lived experience*. This is a book about harnessing the power of the live encounter between students and teachers. It is intended for students who wish to learn more about the theoretical concepts behind the approach, for faculty who might be interested in what experiential education looks like in practice, and for administrators trying to respond programmatically and creatively to a rapidly changing landscape in higher education. If Tyler Hall and the new Phase Two building outside my window represent anything, I think they represent the tensions in the academy between that which is eternal and enduring, and that which is ephemeral and ever-changing. This is a particularly challenging time period to prognosticate in higher education, but I do think there is one thing I can safely say—that opportunities to be fully present with others will continue to be valued and will continue to stand the test of time as one of the chief values and aims of liberal education. The live encounter can and should endure.

OUTLINE AND STRUCTURE OF THIS BOOK

Experiential Education in the College Context consists of two main parts and eight chapters: Part 1 delves into the conceptual category itself—how we might come to think about Dewey's "educative experience" and how it represents a distinctive approach to the questions of the purposes of education and what knowledge is of the most worth. It is important to me, as a philosopher of education, to explore these more theoretical issues alongside questions of practice. Too often, particularly in the field of experiential education, questions of theory are overlooked in the desire to talk about practice. But skipping over theory on the way to application is fraught with peril. As we shall see, there are a variety of ways one might employ experiential education depending on deeper, philosophical stances in education. Decontextualizing experiential education and simply applying it as a technique can do real harm.

On the other hand, we must also be cautious not to overdo conceptual complexity to the point we forget about the importance of actual application. Often referred to as "paralysis by analysis," one can get bogged down in a sort of quest for certainty about what, finally, experiential education "is." This is why I have chosen in this book to put both theory and practice together. Thus, in addition to discussing how we come to conceive of experiential education and its various curricular projects, I also lift up and discuss specific applications of the approach currently in practice in higher education. Organized around four broad categories: active learning, integrated learning, project-based learning, and community-based learning, these categories serve as a way to organize the "ecosystem" of methodologies within experiential education. The categories themselves are surely not the only way to organize and discuss experiential education on the college campus but they are mine and one has to begin from some kind of typology to get started.

In Part 2 of the book, I explore the principles and practices held in common between all the various methodologies and approaches. From pedagogical stance, to questions of design, facilitation, and assessment, these chapters are intended to give the reader specific and practical suggestions on the road to teaching more experientially. These principles and practices are mostly gleaned from my personal experience working in this field over the last twenty years; some are concepts of my own, many are not. I have attempted to attribute where I can, but many of these principles and practices are now so wrapped up in years of practice and iterative change that I cannot remember where they came from originally. What I can say is that they have helped me tremendously as I work with college students. And, when I have given workshops to other faculty, I have heard them say that they have helped them, too.

The final chapter of the book returns to the bigger perspective of where experiential education fits within larger movements within the university. Here, I discuss strategies for a more integrated and comprehensive approach to experiential education across the institution—moving it from shallow and isolated practice to a deep and pervasive ethos. This, of course, is highly context dependent and I don't pretend to know or have a one-size-fits-all approach to institutional change. The lessons I discuss in this section are admittedly broad brush, but my hope is that they can provide a useful point of departure for the work on your campus.

REFERENCES

Arendt, H. (1958). *The Human Condition*. Chicago, IL: University of Chicago Press.

Green, M. (1988). *The Dialectic of Freedom*. New York: Teachers College.

REFERENCES

Foreword

THE PERSONAL ENCOUNTER MAY BE OUR LAST AND ONLY REASON TO EXIST

For the privileged few of us who work in academia, the current sensations of wandering in the wilderness are the result of once-in-a-generation disruptions to every aspect of our business. The wilderness that we are wandering through is vastly different than the one we successfully traversed to get to our present locations and, as a result, much of the previous wayfinding we have done in the past is not helpful in this new context.

When I was obtaining my Bachelor of Arts in English and History in the late 1980s, it was not necessary nor expected that any of my professors would do anything beyond share their content expertise in Milton, Shakespeare, or Nazi Germany, and most of our encounters were entirely one-way despite small class sizes. It was fine for them to simply show up, mentally hit "play" on their lecture playlist, and divulge in depth about the niche topics they had devoted their lives to. At that time, there were no administrative or governmental directives to draw any employability connections between writing an essay comparing two of the Bard's sonnets to "real world" situations of analyzing two loan applications at the bank. No, my time in those English and History classrooms was less about me and what I would be able to do with my degree and more about the professors' particular platforms. It wasn't until I was six months into a position as a legislative assistant for a U.S. Senator that I had actually learned the job-worthy skills of analysis, critical thinking, communication, and historical context.

While all education is experiential by the nature of experiencing something, even in a non-interactive lecture, Professor Roberts and others suggest that "true" experiential education provides teachers and students with opportunities to frame the content within a relevant and applicable context. That is not to say that it is always easy to create or find those opportunities but there is no discipline or topic or content that is out of reach. As students, parents, policy makers, and politicians (aka the funders of most higher education) become increasingly more astute and discerning about the value of a college degree, it is incumbent on us to invoke the experiential models whose origins stem back to the ancient Greeks and re-establish the relevance of what we are doing.

A NEED FOR RELATIONSHIPS

In addition to needing hope and faith that my BA degree of the 1980s would be relevant to the world beyond my leafy campus at that time, I could only receive such a degree by being on the leafy campus. Before the University of Phoenix, MOOCs, Course Management Systems, class blogs, podcasts, and PowerPoint slides, acquiring a diploma and supposedly unlocking the gates of a better life, required being mentally and physically present in a shared space with the teacher and other students. While I know that there were correspondence degrees available at the time, their popularity, uptake, and credibility was minimal. Thus, the whole premise of higher education rested on the personal encounter and the classroom experience. As noted above, although these encounters were often one-way transmissions on somewhat arcane matters of importance to the teachers, they did require some kind of personal engagement between teacher, student, and content.

With the advent of ubiquitous educational technology, that three-part formula has now been shattered into discrete pieces of teaching, learning, content, and assessment whereby a student can obtain those pieces in different places. Take a recent MOOC (Massive Online Open Course) that I participated in as a student. The content, positive psychology, was provided in the form of short (10–20 minutes), topic-focused, any time available videocasts delivered over two months by three experts located in different parts of the U.S. Readings in the form of articles, research reports, and excerpts from books were provided online and "discussions" took place among the 10,000 students in self-regulated forums, chat rooms, message threads, and blogs. The assessment for the course was voluntary and was the only portion that cost anything if you wanted it graded (i.e. $25 for the first assignment, $50 for the second, and $100 for the third) in order to receive a certificate of completion. I did not opt for the paid assessment as I drifted away ("dropped out") from the course within two weeks. Why?

My educational background and therefore my educational future is predicated on the personal encounter that only comes through being physically and mentally present during the learning experience. Even in those instances where the teaching has been completely didactic, being immersed within the milieu of teaching, learning, and content is more engaging to me than trying to piece together disparate parts collected elsewhere. However, I recognize that the Red Box/Netflix generation (myself included) is now willing to trade that personal encounter with a knowledgeable video store employee for lower prices and more choices unless the store encounter provides us with something we can't get otherwise—a hearty recommendation for a film that the worker knows I will like based on our previous conversations or waiving late fees or sideways suggestions of novels and places to eat. Decisions driving the delivery and financial models for higher education are not far behind what has happened to the rental video industry. Unless we provide students, parents, politicians, and institutional leaders with clear answers as to why it is still worthwhile to invest in the physical plant of a campus despite easy and more affordable access to online education through a laptop and Internet connection, we are working ourselves toward obsolescence.

When wandering in any kind of wilderness, guidebooks can be key. They can orient us, help discern pathways forward, and educate on the specifics of a place. As experiential initiatives on college and university campuses continue to grow and develop, it is critical that practitioners and scholars alike find common ground, establish new trailheads, and map the terrain ahead. In our present state of disruption, Professor Roberts has provided a very useful text for the wayfinding ahead.

Dr. Billy O'Steen, Associate Professor in Community Engagement
Director, UC Community Engagement Hub
University of Canterbury
Christchurch, New Zealand

Acknowledgments

This project has been a dream of mine for quite some time, so to be at the end of a process that began as the seed of an idea about three years ago is especially gratifying. It also makes me grateful for the support of many people who helped along the way. I would like to thank especially my colleagues at Earlham who have served as sounding boards (and sometimes guinea pigs) to various thoughts and ideas about experiential education over the years. Someone once gave me the advice always to surround yourself with people who are better than you are, and then work like the dickens to try to keep up—that is certainly the case with the collection of colleagues I have the privilege to work with at Earlham. I would also particularly like to thank the staff of the Center for Integrated Learning for their support, encouragement, and hard work which allowed me the space I needed to get this project done. I could not have done this without you. To my wife, I owe many debts of gratitude for your patience, your good critical reading eye, and your uncanny ability to keep me (and seemingly everyone else in your life) on track. And to my students, past, present, and future—outside of my wife and children, you are my greatest joy in this world. Your questions, your passion, and your spirit drive me everyday to be the best I can be in your presence. Thank you.

One of the greatest experiences in writing this book was the opportunity I had to talk with so many inspiring educators and university administrators across higher education. As I conducted interviews, discussed pedagogy, and bounced ideas for innovation off of these folks, I was constantly impressed with their insights, their ingenuity, and their determination. I would particularly like to thank the colleagues who assisted with this project through agreeing to be interviewed including Susan Ambrose, Mary Louise Bringle, Karlyn Crowley, Art Heinricher, Matthew Johnson, Megan Keiser, Jeffrey Plank, Billy Osteen, Maria Stein, and Elly Vandergrift. I would also like to express my gratitude to many fellow experientialists who have inspired me along the way, including Mark Voorhees at the University of Virginia for your longstanding mentorship, support, and role modeling; my colleague and friend Jayson Seaman at the University of New Hampshire for the many conversations about the philosophies of experiential education we have had over the years; to Arianne Hoy and Bobby Hackett at the Bonner Foundation for modeling what best practices look like in community-based learning; and to Billy O'Steen for agreeing to write the Foreword to this book, for your inspirational work at the University of Canterbury, and for your friendship. There are many, many more teachers and facilitators I have worked with over the years—too many to acknowledge here. But each encounter and interaction has had an influence on me and on this book.

Finally, I would also like to thank the editorial staff at Routledge for taking such good care of me and this book project, in particular Heather Jarrow, Samuel Huber, and Karen Adler.

PART 1

The Landscape of Experiential Education

Chapter 1

Introduction

And Max's room grew and grew until the walls became the world all around.

(Maurice Sendak, from *Where the Wild Things Are*)

THE GREAT DISRUPTION

On February 22, 2011, my wife and I had just arrived back at our apartment in Christchurch, New Zealand, after picking up our youngest daughter from daycare. We were in New Zealand leading a semester study abroad program for the college where I worked as a professor of education and environmental studies. On this particular Tuesday, our students were out at their assigned internship sites spread all across the city so we had the day mostly "off" (although anyone who has ever led an off-campus semester program knows that there is no such thing as a "day off"). It was a calm, clear, and beautiful late summer afternoon in New Zealand—one of those rare days with little wind, comfortable temperatures, and sunny skies on the South Island where you truly feel blessed to be alive.

It happened so fast and so violently that I can't really remember what I was thinking or doing. One moment I was standing near the door looking at my wife in the kitchen and the next moment the entire apartment began to shake as if a giant had just picked up the building and rattled it around to see if anything would fall out of it. This was no gentle, swaying earthquake but rather a short, sharp, shock that lasted less than 15 seconds. But in that short period of time, everything changed.

We later found out that this event was technically an aftershock of the September 4, 2010 7.1 magnitude earthquake that struck the region. While this aftershock only measured 6.3 on the Richter scale, comparing the two events with this metric can be very misleading. The February 22 event had the highest Peak Ground Acceleration (PGA) in New Zealand's history and was one of the greatest ever recorded in the world. This acceleration, had it happened in other cities in the world, would have had devastating consequences—flattening most buildings. New Zealand's strict building codes minimized the destruction as much as possible, but the tremor still caused 185 fatalities and reduced the city center to rubble.

In the shock of such moments, you begin to take in the enormity in isolated chunks and snapshots from the senses. First came simple visuals—our daughter, terrified, in my wife's arms. The refrigerator contents smashed and spilled all over the kitchen floor. The television, broken, lying on the carpet. Then came sounds. Car alarms, sounding off somewhere in the distance. A dog barking. An eery silence where there was once bird song and traffic. But eventually, you return to the integrated whole of it and begin to take stock. The enormity of the situation floods in the way water breaks through a failed levy. What about our oldest daughter who was in school? Are we safe remaining in this building? What about all our students? The water was off, the electricity was out, the landline was cut, and cell service was non-existent. In an instant, we went from a calm, relaxing, sunny afternoon to a disaster zone the magnitude of which was only just settling in. We felt isolated, out of contact, unprepared, and vulnerable.

In a very real sense, those of us who work in higher education are experiencing a similar predicament. Living through our own "Great Disruption," colleges and universities in the United States and across the world are attempting to come to grips with several seismic shocks that have left many in the academy feeling isolated, vulnerable, and unprepared. It is not within the scope of this particular book to go into great detail about the present socio-cultural context of higher education of which much has been written. Derek Bok's (2009) *Our Underachieving Colleges*, Vince Ferrall's (2011) *Liberal Arts on the Brink*, Arum and Roksa's (2011), *Academically Adrift: Limited Learning on College Campuses*, and Andrew Delbanco's (2014) *College: What It Was, Is, and Should Be,* all reveal a host of issues and challenges with the current state of the academy. And, it should be noted, this particular period may not be as unique as we think. A cursory glance at the history of higher education would reveal other time periods of turmoil and existential questioning. Heeding this, some have come to the defense of the traditional liberal arts as noted in recent works by Michael Roth (2014) *Beyond the University: Why Liberal Education Matters* and Fareed Zakaria (2015) *In Defense of a Liberal Education.* Nonetheless, it is hard to argue that this particular time period, just following the turn of the century, feels particularly disruptive in terms of its affects. As Delbanco states:

> The role of faculty is changing everywhere, and no college is impervious to the larger forces that, depending on one's point of view, promise to transform, or threaten to undermine, it. As these forces bear down on us, neither lamentation nor celebration will do. Instead, they seem to me to compel us to confront some basic questions about the purposes and possibilities of college education.
>
> (2012, p. 6)

As Delbanco argues, the current disruption is not a simple "good:bad" binary. But stating this does not suggest, in my view, that those of us working in higher education should just sit back and wait for the dust to settle. Every crisis brings along with it opportunity.

I recently returned to Christchurch and spent the better part of an afternoon wandering the city center, almost three years after the earthquake. Driving downtown was disorienting to the extreme. City streets were unrecognizable as I looked in vain for familiar landmarks and buildings to help feel my way into town. After several wrong turns, I finally parked the car in one of the many gravel lots that now take the place of where office buildings used to stand. The contrast to what I remember was shocking. Cashel Street, the Bus Exchange, Victoria Park—all of these landmarks were fundamentally altered. Some locations were in the midst of construction and rebuilding. Others seemed to exist in a kind of time capsule—shattered glass, store front signs, and barricades remained just as they were on that February day three years ago. One memorable block had a chain link fence surrounding a closed series of storefronts seemingly open and ready for business. A "keep out" sign hung half-off its hinges on the fence.

Walking past yet another empty gravel lot where a building once stood, I paused. Instead of a weed-choked and depressingly empty space, this lot had what appeared to be an amphitheater and art installation made out of pallets. The pallets formed a kind of temporary building with space for live music, a café with free wifi, and a place for people to gather and socialize. A sign nearby explained this was one of many such "gap-filler" art installations and projects spread throughout the city center in response to the many empty gravel lots I had been seeing. These projects were dreamed up and installed by artists and citizens coming together and, as Maxine Greene (1988) once wrote, "imagining things otherwise" amidst tragedy, devastation, and loss. Moving through the city, my mood changed from sorrow and pity to a sense of admiration for the

5

grit, resilience, and determination of the citizens of Christchurch. Cashel Mall—once the pulsing center of the city—had been completed destroyed by the earthquake. In its place, a "container mall" has sprung up lined with stores operating out of shipping containers to create a funky, and quite effective, retail zone.

As I got back in my car and drove away, it struck me that the city was an illustrative example of the choices we make in the midst of disruption. We can, like some of the abandoned buildings and cordoned-off areas of a city, simply pretend the disruption never occurred in the first place, posting metaphorical "keep out" signs and cordoning off our college campuses from critique and calls for reform. Clinging to what we remember of the past, there is a certain relief and comfort knowing that, even if damaged, things still look familiar. We can also, like the gap-filler projects, use the disruption as an open-space of creative expression. Although some new installations will likely fail, or will last only for a short period of time, the acts of collaboration and expression will likely yield new ideas, long-term benefits, and even structural change. And all this disruption and innovation is happening at a compressed pace. As Bass (2012) noted:

> Our understanding of learning has expanded at a rate that has far outpaced our conceptions of teaching. A growing appreciation for the porous boundaries between the classroom and life experience, along with the power of social learning, authentic audiences, and integrative contexts, has created not only promising changes in learning but also disruptive moments in teaching.
>
> (p. 24)

Of course, higher education is not comparable to a devastated city. Across our campuses we could all point to both hopeful and dismaying "city blocks" and we might not even agree on which is which. The future ahead of us is not a simple choice between stasis and transformation. But, it is important to recognize, as Bass states above, that the changes being experienced are simultaneously promising and threatening, and provoke us to ask hard questions about the nature of teaching and learning in the 21st century.

And, in this particular disruptive moment in higher education, these questions can invite us to consider the role of experiential education in generating potential answers. There are a variety of ways that colleges and universities are attempting to exhibit both adaptation and resilience given these disruptive forces. This book explores one particular phenomenon—the rise of experiential learning initiatives across higher education. As someone who has spent a good deal of time practicing experiential teaching and learning in higher education, I am convinced that it can serve as not only a "gap-filler" but as an essential creative force during this time of disruption. However, as a student and scholar on curriculum theory and the philosophy of education, I am keenly aware (and skeptical) of panacea pedagogical pronouncements. I highlight this particular curricular response not because I believe it is the only response but because I firmly believe it is a good response and a useful one. Any philosopher of education will rightly shy away from universalistic claims of pedagogical purity. It has never been my stance to claim that experiential approaches are, by definition, the best in a given educational context. But, given this particular historical moment, and this particular generation of students, and this particular time of societal need, I *do* believe experiential education is worth paying more attention to. And, that higher education has been slow to pick up on the pedagogical power of experience (something the K–12 world has been much quicker to incorporate). As Moore (2013) wrote:

> [M]any faculty members, if they think about experiential education at all, regard it with disdain, or they grudgingly tolerate it because it generates enrollments. Moreover . . . programs tend to be located at the institutional margins, not in the core academic units.

So, this is *not* a book about how experiential education will save the academy. It is not a book claiming that the only effective way to teach and learn is through experiential approaches. There is too much history that demonstrates the folly of any grand, universalizing declarations of this-or-that "new method." John Dewey himself, the so-called "father" of experiential education, was known to lecture quite frequently as a professor in college. This is also not a book about applying experiential education as the one and only effective method available to a teacher. In fact, seeing experiential education as *method* is a large part of the problem (which we will discuss in more detail in Chapter 2). Rather, this book approaches the current disruption as an opportunity to, as Delbanco (2012) states, "question the purposes and possibilities of a college education" *and* to give some practical tools for enacting experiential curricula that I have learned along the way.

SEISMIC SHIFTS

When Thomas Friedman described the world as "flat" in 2005, it was a clarifying moment in how we viewed the intersecting dynamics of globalization and digital technology. Regardless of one's theoretical stance on globalization, it is difficult to argue against the notion that the Internet and subsequent rapid rise in technological innovation has been nothing short of a new "Gutenburg Press" moment for humankind. And, just as during Johannes Gutenberg's time, this new era challenges existing structures to adapt to a rapidly changing landscape. As Friedman noted in 2006:

> To put it another way, the experiences of the high-tech companies in the last few decades that failed to navigate the rapid changes brought about in their marketplace by these types of forces may be a warning to all business, institutions, and nation-states that are now facing these inevitable, even predictable, changes but lack the leadership, flexibility, and imagination to adapt—not because they are not smart or aware, *but because the speed of change is simply overwhelming them.*
>
> (p. 49, emphasis added)

We are more global, connected, and interdependent than ever before. Distance learning, video conferencing, crowd sourcing, social media, and the extreme individualization and portability of learning continue to send aftershocks throughout K–12 and higher education.

It is also worth noting how fast this has come about. It is not just change, as Friedman notes above, it is the combined pace and quality of the change that is so disruptive—to continue the analogy from the Christchurch earthquake, its "Peak Ground Acceleration." Just 20 years ago, when I was in college, there was hardly a public Internet, a "digital device" would probably mean a calculator, and the only phones we had were the landlines installed in the dorm hallway. The vernacular on college and universities campuses today would be incomprehensible to college faculty and students of the 1990s— "twitter feeds," "facebook," "social media," "selfies," "Moodle," "wireless," "tablets" . . . the list could go on and on. And this change is not limited to higher education—the landscape of primary and secondary schooling is also shifting rapidly as a result of new learning technologies. As Bowen (2012) notes:

> One million high school students were enrolled in online courses in 2007, and that number is growing even more rapidly than enrollment in college online courses . . . One study at Harvard predicts that half of all high school courses will be delivered online by 2019
>
> (pp. 8–9)

This accelerated change means we now have a generation of students moving up through the system *expecting* to experience some degree of online learning in college.

The current poster child for the speed of these disruptive forces is the "MOOC" (Massive Open Online Course). Without wading too deep into the debate around MOOCs, it is worth noting that the virtual hysteria they have generated is less about the actual promises or limitations of this new online learning approach and more about how MOOCs embody (or not) the deeper cracks and fissures in the foundations of higher education as a result of the digital age. I remember when the "Palm Pilot" came out in the early part of the 2000s. Everyone seemed to be using one to manage their calendar and to-do lists. Today, all of them exist in attics, dusty drawers, or ten feet down in the municipal landfill. One could take a lesson from this to ignore all this technological fetishization given that there will always be another revolutionary device to come along and "transform" our lives. However, I think that would be a mistake. The Palm Pilot and its ilk were not just another example of shallowness, consumerism, and planned obsolescence (although they certainly were at least that). It was a harbinger. A harbinger of what has now dramatically changed society—the handheld device (tablets and smartphones). If we had been paying close attention during the Palm Pilot phase, those devices were giving us a window into our future. In the same sense, MOOCs may or may not "transform" higher education in the ways some believe it will. But, like Palm Pilots, I believe if we pay close attention, MOOCs are a harbinger of change. Bowen argues:

> The point here is not that online learning is better but just that it is here. Outside of traditional higher education, online resources have been transformative; you can already become a pilot, pharmacist, veterinarian, lawyer, or rabbi online . . . The breadth of technologies, the capabilities of recent software, and the amount of free content will surprise most faculty . . . As long as these technologies expand what we already do (and since most don't threaten traditional colleges), we can probably be convinced to use online resources as a supplement. This tepid embrace, however, will change . . . A large global market wants cheap, high-quality, online education, and American students increasingly want more flexibility and convenient schedules. Someone will meet that demand.
>
> (p. 9)

Whether or not MOOCs really do represent a paradigm shift in higher education is almost beside the point. The deeper reality is that we are experiencing our own "Gutenburg Press" moment with the advent of digital technology—it is increasingly embedded into our daily lives and will be even more so for the foreseeable future.

Another seismic disruption in higher education is the destabilization of the "formal" curriculum. As we continue the shift away from a paradigm of instruction to one of student learning, the former power centers on college and university campuses (classrooms, courses, disciplines) are increasingly questioned. As Barr and Tagg wrote in 1995:

> A paradigm shift is taking hold in American higher education. In its briefest form, the paradigm that has governed our colleges is this: A college is an institution that exists to provide instruction. Subtly but profoundly, we are shifting to a new paradigm: A college is an institution that exists to produce learning. This shift changes everything. It is both needed and wanted.
>
> (p. 12)

Twenty years later, Barr and Tagg's analysis rings true. If the rise of digital technologies represents a "Gutenburg Press" moment for us in higher education, the shift in emphasis from the instructional paradigm to the student learning paradigm represents a corresponding "Copernican Turn." The learning universe of an undergraduate no longer revolves exclusively around the formal curriculum. The new center is student learning—wherever it may occur. To Bass (2012):

> We might say that the formal curriculum is being pressured from two sides. On the one side is a growing body of data about the power of experiential learning in the co-curriculum; and on the other side is the world of informal learning and the participatory culture of the Internet. Both of those pressures are reframing what we think of as the formal curriculum. These pressures are disruptive because to this point we have funded and structured our institutions as if the formal curriculum were the center of learning, whereas we have supported the experiential co-curriculum (and a handful of anomalous courses, such as first-year seminars) largely on the margins, even as they often serve as the poster children for the institutions' sense of mission, values, and brand. All of us in higher education need to ask ourselves: Can we continue to operate on the assumption that the formal curriculum is the center of the undergraduate experience?
>
> (p. 24)

This decentering challenges many of the historic structures of the university itself—both physical and epistemological. The academic building of today on a college campus, for example, is relatively unchanged from the beginnings of university concept itself. The University of Bologna, in Italy, is generally considered to be the oldest continual university in the world having been established in 1088. Paintings from early European university classrooms don't look all that unfamiliar to us today—a professor situated in front of a room with a lectern and students seated in rows with paper and quill. From the beginning, universities were physical places with buildings and classrooms wedded to instructional activity and faculty who lectured on the classical disciplines of the trivium (logic, rhetoric, and grammar) and the quadrivium (arithmetic, geometry, music, and astronomy). Early colleges in the United States like Harvard, Yale, and Princeton were organized and designed to "re-create a little bit of old England in America." They wished "to found themselves a college, an English college such as those they had known at Oxford . . . [and] . . . Cambridge" (Rudolph, p. 4, 1990). It is an interesting reflection on cross-cultural patterns on planet Earth that, regardless of where one may be in the world today—China, Brazil, England, South Africa, New Zealand, or the United States—the modern college or university classroom and curriculum looks virtually identical. No matter the cultural differences and distinctions of those widely varying places, when you step foot in the university building, sit down in a college classroom, or peruse the academic offerings, you immediately recognize its familiarity. For the last several centuries we have had a common, relatively unchanged, picture of what the undergraduate experience looks like—both in terms of its physical location and in terms of the intellectual activity that occurs there. H. G. Wells once said: "We are living in 1937, and our universities, I suggest, are not half-way out of the fifteenth century. We have made hardly any changes in our conception of university organization, education, graduation, for a century—for several centuries" (Doss, 2015).

One of the reasons the present period is so disruptive is that it challenges both the physical *and* intellectual structures of the university system. We created campuses, we built buildings, and we organized schedules entirely around majors, courses, and classrooms as the center of teaching and learning. To Bass (2012):

> [O]ne key source of disruption in higher education is coming not from the outside but from our own practices, from the growing body of experiential modes of learning, moving from margin to center, and proving to be critical and powerful in the overall quality and meaning of the undergraduate experience. As a result, at colleges and universities we are running headlong into our own structures, into the way we do business.
>
> (p. 25)

These structures have typically revolved around the classroom as a physically situated place for learning. "Make sure you go to class" is the common advice given. "Class" in this sense is a physical place that one had to "go" to. It is a room with tables, chairs, blackboards, and four walls. When students would plead with their professor on a nice fall or spring day to "have class outside" they meant something quite specific. And, on those lucky occasions when the professor agreed, students would pick up their things, head out to a nice green patch of grass, sit down, and essentially do the same kinds of things they would have done inside (except typically, with more distractions). We find ourselves today, for the first time since the inception of the university concept itself, with a challenge to this model. "Having class outside" today means much more than simply a little fresh air on a lawn. "Having class outside" now means locating learning outside the traditional structures of the physical classroom and the formal curriculum. There are many examples of this shift. The increased usage of Learning Management Systems such as Moodle or Blackboard, and the veritable explosion of e-portfolio platforms all allow for facilitated learning activity outside the physically located classroom. The rise of the term "flipped classroom"—where students watch a video-based lecture on their own and come to a physically located classroom to discuss speaks to this blending of "inside" and "outside" learning. The integration of the curriculum and "co-curriculum" point to the growing realization that students spend far more of their time *outside* the classroom than in it and it might be wise to try and capitalize on these learning spaces. Yet another example is the rise of off-campus learning opportunities. From internships and externships to service learning and study abroad, learning is happening outside the traditional classroom and curriculum infrastructure and off the campus boundaries.

And, of course, the most radical example of all is the non-physically located college or university campus. Students today can get associate degrees, bachelor's, master's, and even Ph.D.s entirely online, without ever having to step foot in a traditional classroom environment. Whether this is a good or bad thing is debatable, but for now, suffice it to say, the physically situated classroom and curriculum, despite its dominance over the centuries, is being destabilized like no other time in history. Microsoft founder Bill Gates put it bluntly when he said:

Place-based colleges are good for parties, but are becoming less crucial for learning thanks to the Internet . . . Five years from now on the Web for free you'll be able to find the best lectures in the world. It will be better than any single university . . . College, except for the parties, needs to be less place-based.

(Young, 2010)

As locations for learning become decentered from physical classrooms, challenging questions are being asked about the value and effectiveness of bricks and mortar campuses. The significance of Gates's use of the word "place" here is not to be overlooked. The college or university as a physical concrete reality, as not just a *space* but a *place* is under significant and sustained critique. Are we rapidly moving into a model of the "University of Nowhere"?

It is no wonder, then, given these seismic shifts combined with the rising costs of a college degree, that the last decade has seen increased criticism, skepticism, and existential angst over the current state of higher education. A cursory review of recent stories in the popular press illustrates how this skepticism has reverberated out of the academy and into the public discourse— from "Envisioning a Post-Campus America" (*Atlantic*, February 2012) to "We're Ripe for a Great Disruption in Higher Education" (*Globe and Mail*, 2012), and, "The Imminent Shake-Out? Disruptive Innovation and Higher Education" (Lenox, 2013), it is clear that higher education is experiencing an intense period of critical examination. In a (2015) online article in *Forbes* titled "Our Universities Are Not Teaching Innovation," Henry Doss argues:

> Not only are our universities not teaching innovation or delivering an innovation experience, they seem to be doing their best to destroy innovative thinking in young people . . . Business leaders, politicians and economists all say more or less the same thing: The future depends on innovation and without it we are doomed as a country and a society to second-class status . . . But what kind of learning experience do we present to university and college students? From the day they set foot on a campus, most students are greeted with a homogenized, pre-packaged, profoundly compartmentalized, deeply siloed, interest-entrenched world. The experience of the modern university system is the antithesis of innovative leadership traits.

While there is clearly a certain amount of "piling on" at this particular historical and cultural moment in criticizing the modern university system (some of it unjustified or uninformed), it nonetheless seems clear that for a variety of complex and interdependent reasons, the ground beneath U.S. colleges and universities is shifting dramatically. These Gutenberg and Copernican turns combined with the rapid rise in the cost of higher education, a post-recession economy that has struggled to produce jobs, and a shrinking middle class have produced an existential threat like none other to the modern university system as we have come to know it.

13

THE POSSIBILITIES OF THE LIVE ENCOUNTER

Yet, despite the stereotypical popular press images of the wizened, grey-bearded professor lecturing in front of a vast sea of bored co-eds, teaching and learning in higher education *is changing* and one aspect of that change is the increased usage of experiential approaches. All across the United States and in other parts of the world, in community colleges, small liberal arts colleges, and major research universities, we find students, faculty, and staff engaging in various forms of experiential "deep play." Some of these initiatives are born from longstanding historical curriculum projects (such as cooperative education, or the work college model) and are not "new" per se. Others have only just emerged in the last decade or so (such as game-based learning). The number and variety of these initiatives are noteworthy—from the rise of off-campus study programs and internships, to the increased use of the community as a location for student research and projects, to campus gardens, and the development of complex problem-based simulations and project-based learning, there is a strong streak of pedagogical experimentation occurring on and off campus. The premise behind this book is that much of this deep play has a common taproot, what John Dewey (1938) termed "educative experience." While some may see these initiatives and activities as somewhat faddish, their popularity and success point to new forms[1] of teaching and learning—forms that are more active, relevant, problem-based, collaborative, complex, and interdisciplinary.

But what about experiential education makes it worth trying in the college context? Why should the average faculty member or administrator care? I think there are both philosophical and evidence-based reasons to take experiential education seriously. Philosophically, experiential education facilitates what Parker Palmer termed the "live encounter." To Palmer (1998):

> Academic institutions offer myriad ways to protect ourselves from the threat of the live encounter. To avoid a live encounter with teachers, students can hide behind their notebooks and their silence. To avoid a live encounter with students, teachers can hide behind their podiums, their credentials, their power . . . To avoid a live encounter with subjects of study, teachers and students alike can hide behind the pretense of objectivity: students can say, "Don't ask me to think about this stuff—just give me the facts," and faculty can say, "Here are the facts—don't think about them, just get them straight."
>
> (p. 37)

The live encounter in education gets beyond the script, the expected, the given, and the predictable. To do so is perhaps the most robust definition of liberal education and yet much of what students experience in the classroom fails on this account. Matthew Crawford, author of *Shop Class as Soulcraft*, recounts a telling example when he describes "Build-a-Bear"—a popular store in shopping malls.

> One of the hottest things at the shopping mall right now is a store called Build-a-Bear, where children are said to make their own teddy bears. I went into one of these stores, and it turns out that what the kid actually does is select the features and clothes for the bear on a computer screen, then the bear is made for him. Some entity has *leaped in* ahead of us and taken care of things already, with a kind of solicitude. The effect is to preempt cultivation of embodied agency, the sort that is natural to us.
>
> (2009, p. 69, emphasis in text)

The Build-a-Bear is the opposite of the live encounter. While the situation presents itself as the ultimate expressions of choice and freedom, they are mere illusions. As Crawford states, "some entity has leaped in ahead of us and taken care of things . . . the effect is to preempt cultivation of embodied agency, the sort that is natural to us." Too much of what goes on in higher education today looks like "Build-a-Bear" to me—scripted classrooms, scripted majors, and scripted lives—even as students experience enumerable "choices" within existing structures. If we are truly going to use this current disruption to question the "purposes and possibilities of a college education" as Delbanco suggests, then I believe we must revitalize the live encounter between students and teachers on our campuses.

However, what about experiential education helps facilitate more live encounters? In Martin Jay's *Songs of Experience* (2005), he details the Latin, Greek, and German origins of the term. In it, he explains how "the English word is understood to be derived most directly from the Latin *experientia*, which denoted "trial, proof, or experiment" (p. 10). He goes on to note how the verb "to try" in Italian (*expereri*) shares a root with the word for "peril" or "danger" (*periculum*) which suggests a "covert association between experience and peril [and that experience comes] from having survived risks and learned something from the encounter" (p. 10). This, to me, goes right to the heart of what I think we mean when we evoke the power of experience to facilitate the live encounter. Experiential education done well is *risky*. Setting off outside the campus boundaries for an internship, working together on a community project of real consequence, leaving your home country to study abroad, all these scenarios involve elements of uncertainty, challenge, and complexity—all contain within them the possibility of Palmer's "live encounter" and resist Crawford's "Build-a-Bear." As Jay noted above, experience comes "from having survived risks and learned something from the encounter." Doss (2015) argued that if universities really wanted to teach innovation:

> We'd let students fail. In fact, we'd structure our educational system to be certain they'd fail. We'd let them fail, with serious, real consequences for that failure. We would not shelter them from failure, nor would we shelter them from risk. Lots of risk. The self-confidence and psychic endurance a real innovator must have doesn't come so much from a smooth path toward success, as it does from learning that you can recover from failure. Success is easy. Failure is more important.

Experiential educators design for just these sorts of encounters. Classrooms and learning situations come "alive" when something is at stake—whether that is the personal risk of speaking from experience, the social risk of practicing new knowledge, skills, or abilities in front of others, the pedagogical risk of beginning an activity without predetermined outcomes, or the ethical risk of trying to solve real problems in a community of interest. And such strivings are not simply pedagogically effective (though they are that); they also form the foundation (to Dewey and others) of democratic community. As Maxine Greene (1988) once argued: "It is important to hold in mind the idea (as important for Charles Taylor, Hannah Arendt, and Jurgen Habermas as for Dewey) that the *person*—that center of choice—develops in his/her fullness to the degree he/she is a member of a live community" (emphasis in text, p. 43).

Beyond the more philosophical reasoning, there is an accumulating body of research in teaching and learning to support the effectiveness of more experiential approaches. George Kuh's work on High Impact Practices, for example, demonstrates that experiential approaches have a disproportionate positive impact on student learning. As Kuh (2008) notes "[these] practices have been widely tested and have been shown to be beneficial for college students from many backgrounds" (p. 9). These High Impact Practices include:

- First-year seminars and experiences
- Common intellectual experiences
- Learning communities
- Writing intensive courses

- Collaborative assignments and projects
- Undergraduate research
- Diversity/global learning
- Service learning/community-based learning
- Internships
- Capstone courses and projects.

A cursory glance at this list reveals many teaching and learning practices that are, at their core, *experiential*, including internships, service learning, global learning, learning communities, and collaborative learning. Yet even the practices on this list that don't immediately strike one as experiential can be seen as connected (first-year seminars and experiences, for example). And many of these practices exist *outside* the traditional academic structure of majors and classes. To Bass:

> Many of these practices are not part of the formal curriculum but are in the co-curriculum, or what we used to call the extra-curriculum (e.g., undergraduate research). The rest are special or exceptional curricular experiences (e.g., first-year seminars and capstones). From the perspective of the impact on learning, this intersection of the most learning-intensive experiences in the co-curriculum and in the few exceptional, often experientially focused courses in the formal curriculum forms the new center—the recentered core—of undergraduate learning. Indeed, in my experience of holding focus groups and informal conversations with students, if you ask them where they think their deepest learning has taken place, they will sometimes point to one or two courses that had meaningful impact for them. But they almost always point enthusiastically to the co-curricular experiences in which they invested their time and energy.
>
> (p. 26)

But what is it about *these particular* practices that students find more engaging and effective? Kuh notes that these activities tend to be immersive—students must devote considerable time and effort to purposeful tasks. They require close student–faculty interaction and peer–peer collaboration and relationship building. They place students in diverse and novel contexts where they must engage with the unknown. Practices like these also tend to be "high feedback" in orientation and invite students to integrate across domains. In fact, the research demonstrates that gains are *higher* for students when they participate in multiple high-impact practices across their four years in school. Kuh writes:

17

it can be life changing to study abroad, participate in service learning, conduct research with a faculty member, or complete an internship. That is why doing one or more of these activities in the context of a coherent, academically challenging curriculum that appropriately infuses opportunities for active, collaborative learning increases the odds that students will be prepared to—in the words of William Cronon—"just connect."

(2008, p. 17)

Yet, despite all these positive attributes, experiential education remains on the margins of what goes on in higher education. Kuh notes that "utilization of active learning practices is unsystematic, to the detriment of student learning" (p. 9). Changing that requires acknowledgment of the seismic and disruptive forces affecting the 21st-century college and university, and a comprehensive effort to place student *experience* (and not content instruction) at the center of an institutions academic mission. Experiential education holds the "possibility" of the live encounter for college and university campuses but it is no guarantee. My hope is that this book encourages faculty and administrators to think deeper and more systematically about the role of experiential education in academia. The possibilities are limitless for more live encounters between students, teachers, and subjects of study. All we have to do is be willing to accept the risks that come with that journey.

CONCLUSION

The quotation that begins this chapter is a favorite of mine from all the way back into my childhood. I can remember my father reading this book to me and telling me how much I reminded him of Max. In Sendak's telling of the story, Max misbehaves and is sent to his room where "Max's room grew and grew until the walls became the world all around." The walls of the pre-21st-century university have long been considered "givens"—the campus boundaries, the "academic" buildings, and the four-walled classrooms. But, in a very real sense, the 21st-century university walls are quickly becoming "the world all around." Experiential education, at its most robust, extends the campus, extends the learning, and extends the relationships far beyond our 20th-century structures.

While this is a time of disruption and destabilization, it is also a time of tremendous opportunity in higher education. A central premise of liberal learning is the notion, from Roth (2014), that higher education "should be able to teach students to liberate, animate, cooperate, and instigate. Through doubt, imagination, and hard work, students come to understand that they really can reshape themselves and their societies" (p. 195). But can we say this not just about our students but also demonstrate it ourselves as teachers, administrators, and institutions of higher education? Can we embrace the possibilities of the live encounter? We know from both natural and cultural systems that times of disruption place a premium on two things: adaptation and resilience. Systems that are stressed must have within them the ability to both change and to recover quickly from difficulties. The question at the center of this book, then, is: What role can (and should) experiential education play in helping the 21st-century university to respond to these disruptive forces?

NOTE

1. It is certainly the case that many of these approaches are not necessarily new— any student of early 20th-century progressive education will recognize elements of the experiential pedagogy. Many K-12 schools such as Expeditionary Learning and Place-Based Learning schools are incorporating these pedagogical principles. Yet I would contend that these sorts of progressive educational approaches have been slower to gain a foothold in higher education.

REFERENCES

Arum, R., & Roksa, J. (2011). *Academically Adrift: Limited Learning on College Campuses.* Chicago, IL: University of Chicago Press.

Barr, R. B., & Tagg, J. (1995). From teaching to learning: A new paradigm for undergraduate education. *Change: The Magazine of Higher Learning, 27*(6), 12–26.

Bass, R. (2012). Disrupting ourselves: The problem of learning in higher education. *Educause Review, 47*(2), 23–33.

Bok, D. (2009). *Our Underachieving Colleges: A Candid Look at How Much Students Learn and Why They Should be Learning More.* Princeton, NJ: Princeton University Press.

Bowen, J. A. (2012). *Teaching Naked: How Moving Technology out of your College Classroom will Improve Student Learning.* San Francisco, CA: Jossey Bass.

Crawford, M. B. (2009). *Shop Class as a Soulcraft: An Inquiry into the Value of Work.* London: Penguin Press.

Delbanco, A. (2014). *College: What it Was, Is, and Should Be.* Princeton, NJ: Princeton University Press.

Dewey, J. (1938). *Experience and Education.* New York: Collier Macmillan.

Doss, H. (2015). Our universities are not teaching innovation. Retrieved February 25, 2015, from: www.forbes.com/sites/henrydoss/2015/02/25/our-universities-are-not-teaching-innovation/

Ferrall, V. E. (2011). *Liberal Arts at the Brink.* Boston, MA: Harvard University Press.

Friedman, T. L. (2006). *The World is Flat: A Brief History of the Twenty-first Century*. New York: Farrar, Straus, & Giroux.

Greene, M. (1988). *The Dialectic of Freedom*. New York: Teachers College.

Jay, M. (2005). *Songs of Experience: Modern American and European Variations on a Universal Theme*. Berkeley, CA: University of California Press.

Kuh, G. D. (2008). *High-impact Educational Practices: What they are, Who has Access to Them, and Why they Matter*. Washington, DC: Association of American Colleges and Universities.

Lenox, M. (2013). *The Imminent Shakeout: Disruptive Innovation and Higher Education*. *Forbes*, March 29. Retrieved from: www.forbes.com/sites/2013/03/29/the-imminent-shakeout-disruptive-innovation-and-higher-education

Mcardle, M. (2012). Envisioning a post-campus America. *The Atlantic*, February 13. Retrieved from: www.theatlantic.com/business/archive/2012/02/envisioning-a-post-campus-america/253032/

Moore, D. T. (2013). For interns, experience isn't always the best teacher. Retrieved March 1, 2015 from: http://chronicle.com/article/For-Interns-Experience-Isnt/143073/

Roth, M. (2014). *Beyond the university: Why liberal education matters*. New Haven, NJ: Yale University Press.

Sendak, M. (1963). *Where the Wild Things Are*. New York: HarperCollins.

Young, J. R. (2010). Bill Gates predicts technology will make "place-based" colleges less important in 5 years. Retrieved September 19, 2013 from: http://chronicle.com/blogs/wiredcampus/bill-gates-predicts-technology-will-make-place-based-colleges-less-important-in-5-years/26092

Zakaria, F. (2015). *In Defense of a Liberal Education*. New York: W. W. Norton & Company.

Chapter 2

Defining Experiential Education

> I would abandon the term "experience" because of my growing realization that the historical obstacles which prevented understanding . . . are, for all practical purposes, insurmountable.
>
> (John Dewey, from *The Later Works,* 1981)

THE QUEST FOR CERTAINTY

When I give talks on experiential education to faculty at various colleges and universities, there comes a point in the question and answer period that I secretly dread. Someone inevitably raises their hand and asks the question that I have spent the better part of my scholarly career trying to work on. "Dr. Roberts," this person asks, "can you give a succinct definition of what actually counts as 'experiential' and what doesn't when it comes to teaching and learning?" This seemingly simple question is fraught with peril. To answer it requires one to either skim the surface or to delve too deeply into philosophical musings on the nature of "experience" and epistemology. Many teachers simply want to know how to operationally define the term "experiential education" so that they can categorize it against other known methodologies such as "lecturing," "discussion," or "group work." Others who are a bit more skeptical hear in the words "experiential" a value statement—that somehow if a teacher is not teaching "experientially" they are doing grave injustices to the students in their care. This has always made answering the question posed a challenge. If I define it methodologically, I risk oversimplifying a complex (and contested) intellectual history. However, if I go too far down the rabbit hole, I leave the audience perplexed and lacking concrete examples to consider in their own pedagogical work.

One thing that gives me recourse in these moments is the fact that I am not alone in struggling with the term. "Experience," as a concept, has flummoxed many of the great philosophers of the ages. Hans-Georg Gadamer (Gadamer & Dutt, 2001) called the concept of experience "one of the most obscure we have" (p. 310). Michael Oakesshott (1933) lamented that "experience, of all the words in the philosophic vocabulary is the most difficult to manage" (p. 9). John Dewey, considered by many to be the most influential philosopher on experiential education, practically gave up on the term in frustration. The quotation that begins this chapter has Dewey arguing that the "historical obstacles which prevent understanding . . . are . . . insurmountable" (1981, p. 361). Given the philosophical complexity of both terms—"experience" and "education"—it is no wonder that many view what Dewey in another context labeled the "quest for certainty" around experiential education as a fool's errand. As one experiential education scholar recently noted in a listserv debate about the "changing nature of experience":

> I have come to see "experience" in a pragmatic way . . . Above all else it serves a social function allowing communicability across differences. I think the logic Herbert Kliebard applies to progressivism fits here (in the epilogue to *Struggle for the American Curriculum*). He maintains "it" [progressivism] never actually existed as a definable thing, but rather serves as a "social language."
>
> (Seaman, 2014, personal communication)

In philosophical terms, I think Seaman is exactly correct here. The term "experiential education" serves as a sort of "tabula rasa" for educators on which to project pedagogical hopes, dreams, fears, and stances. To the extent that there is a "there, there," it is in Kliebard's "social language" and its definitional power is the degree to which that language influences teaching discourse and, by extension, teaching behaviors. And it is worth noting that even that social language is not homogeneous. I have argued in an earlier work (Roberts, 2012) that there is contestation and conflict embedded within notions of experiential education (just as there was and continues to be in progressive education more broadly).

Ah, but perhaps we have strayed too far down the rabbit hole already! But what of the original question? What *counts* as experiential education? Perhaps the pragmatic turn Seaman alludes to above can help here. If we take as a given that the quest for certainty in defining experiential education leads us down a philosophical cul-de-sac, then we are left to focus on teaching and learning *in language and in action*. What do people *say* counts as experiential and what do those curriculum projects look like? I have found Martin Jay's (2005) acceptance of this comforting:

> Rather than force a totalized account, which assumes a unified point of departure, an etymological arche to be recaptured . . . it will be far more productive to follow the disparate threads where they may lead us. Without the burden of seeking to rescue or legislate a single acceptation of the word, we will be free to uncover and explore its multiple and often contradictory meanings and begin to make sense of how and why they function as they often have to produce such powerful effect.
>
> (p. 3)

So, rather than force the "totalized account" that Martin Jay warns of, we will spend the rest of this chapter looking at how the social language of experiential education manifests itself in visible curriculum projects and pedagogy. We will begin with a basic definition[1] of experiential education (one among many) and then explore how this definition plays itself out in three distinct curriculum situations: an internship, a community engagement project, and a game-based simulation. Each situation will build off the previous in terms of what "counts" as experiential education and reveal some of the commonalities, differences, and points of contestation within the field.

DEFINING EXPERIENTIAL EDUCATION

Because one has to start somewhere in terms of defining the social language of experiential education (acknowledging right off the bat that there are many), the definition offered by the Association for Experiential Education (AEE) offers a good enough launching point. According to the AEE, experiential education is

> a philosophy that informs many methodologies in which educators purposefully engage with learners in direct experience and focused reflection in order to increase knowledge, develop skills, clarify values, and develop people's capacity to contribute to their communities.

This definition reveals a key distinction that it would be useful to explore right off the bat. It is the distinction between experiential "education" and experiential "learning." These two terms are often seen—inaccurately in my view—as synonyms. Learning is a process that happens more or less all the time. When we change our son's diaper and get sprayed in the face, we *learn* to make sure that "area" is well covered the next time. When we visit a foreign country we *learn* how to say "hello" and "thank you" in the native tongue. The *Oxford English Dictionary* defines learning as "[t]he acquisition of knowledge or skills through experience, study, or by being taught." Note that the definition includes the phrase "through experience." Much of what we learn we learn through experience. College, in general, involves a whole host of opportunities to acquire "knowledge or skills through experience." If this is the case, then colleges and universities are already doing quite well infusing experiential education into the campus and curriculum. However, we know this is not necessarily the case. And therein lies the difference between experiential *learning* and experiential *education*. Just because someone has learned through experience does not mean that they have done so through experiential education. Again, learning and education are not synonyms. As Itin (1999) argued:

> Meaningful discussions have been . . . hampered in that the terms [experiential education and experiential learning] have been used to describe many different teaching approaches, work experiences, outdoor education, adventure education, vocational education, lab work . . . [and that] experiential education and experiential learning have often been used synonymously with these other terms.
>
> (p. 91)

The *Oxford English Dictionary* defines education as "[t]he process of receiving or giving systematic instruction, especially at a school or university." In this sense, while learning might be considered more informal and individualized, "education" implies a more formal and structured process of teaching and learning. We typically describe colleges and universities as "higher education" because we mean to imply that there is something structured and systematic about the process involved. While there may be a variety of educational contexts that employ experiential *learning*, this does not necessarily mean experiential *education* is a part of the process. What is the difference? Experiential learning is *informal*—one can learn through experience in any number of contexts and curriculum situations. Experiential education involves a broader and more *systematic pedagogical process*. Education, properly conceived, involves important questions about the structure and function of knowledge, the ethical imperatives of such knowledge, and the purposes to which learning ought to adhere.

Thus there is, in fact, a way to do experiential education that is more or less commonly understood and commonly practiced. This is not the case with experiential learning. For example, an Art instructor would probably describe the studio work students complete on painting and drawing as "learning by doing" or learning experientially; or a Chemistry professor might consider the experiments she does in the lab with students as "experiential learning." A coach running a practice on the athletic fields would certainly describe that work with their student-athletes as learning through experience. But in each of these cases, they would likely not describe the overall process as "experiential education." There is certainly "learning by doing" or experiential learning occurring in these situations.

However, it does not necessarily follow that this is the same as the *systematic pedagogical process* of experiential education as articulated by John Dewey (1938) and others. The two ask fundamentally different questions and work in different domains. While this book may refer from time to time to "experiential learning," it is always within the broader pedagogical context of "experiential education." It is not simply about how we learn experientially but rather how we create such moments *through* the systematic processes of experiential education. The following three models will help us explore these processes more concretely.

THREE CURRICULUM MODELS OF EXPERIENTIAL EDUCATION

Curriculum Situation #1: Clarice's Internship

Clarice[2] was really excited for her internship with the Environmental Protection Agency in Washington, DC. As a biology major, she had a passion for science and a desire to explore the intersecting worlds of children's health and public policy. It had always frustrated her that her classes did not explore more real-world issues that demonstrated science in the public sphere. This was her chance to finally *experience* science in a way she didn't feel she had a chance to in the classroom. Working with her faculty advisor, Clarice generated a list of questions that she wanted to explore while working with the EPA. She also created a reading list of articles, books, and resources that would help her better understand the context of her work and how it fit into larger conversations about public health and issues of environmental justice.

While in DC, Clarice met with her supervisor at the EPA to go over expectations and discuss some of the questions she hoped to explore throughout the eight-week internship. Learning goals were written up and agreed upon between her supervisor, Clarice, and her faculty advisor back at school. Several times during her internship, Clarice connected with her advisor, reflecting on what she was learning and doing as well as discussing how her work fit into her larger questions of public policy and science. Clarice returned to school in the fall, met again with her advisor to discuss her learning goals and to prepare for her public Presentation of Learning—a required component of her internship experience. Clarice worked hard on her presentation, integrating her work with the EPA into the readings she was assigned as well as her broader queries about the intersections of science and the public good. Over 50 people showed up for her presentation including members of the biology department, friends, and fellow students. During the question and answer period, Clarice was asked about whether or not she saw Public Health as a possible vocational pathway, about the intersections of race, class, and inequality in her research work, and about her most surprising realization in working for a government agency.

Most teaching faculty reading this curriculum situation would likely describe it as an ideal "educative" experience for Clarice. And, in fact, it was (and based on a true story). But a key question would be: why? Why was it educative? What elements of this curriculum situation came together to ensure that Clarice's experience was successful from an educational standpoint? This particular vignette reveals the oft-cited "experiential learning cycle" articulated by David Kolb (1984).The cycle involves a learner having a concrete experience, reflecting on that experience, forming abstract conceptualizations from that reflection, and then testing out those realizations into new contexts.

Extending Kolb's basic model, experiential educators have often included a "framing" or "pre-exposure" stage prior to the concrete experience (Jensen, 2005; Joplin, 2008). In this particular case, Clarice's internship was "framed" or "pre-exposed" by her coursework, conversations with her faculty advisor, and the questions she generated ahead of time. The concrete experience was the internship itself. Her reflection on that experience was on-going but punctuated by opportunities to discuss what she was experiencing with her supervisor and her faculty advisor. Drawing from those reflections and her readings, Clarice abstracted conceptualizations about the experience as she queried about the intersecting issues of race, class, and inequality in public health policy. Finally, the totality of her experience will influence her future experiences as she tests out new realizations in different contexts and, perhaps, even gain more clarity about possible career pathways.

While Kolb is often the scholar cited for this model, it is worth noting that the basic elements of this learning process have been discussed for some time, most notably by John Dewey but also by other progressive educators such as Maria Montessori, Johan Pestalozzi, Rudolph Steiner, and William Kilpatrick among others. What this particular curriculum situation reveals is the

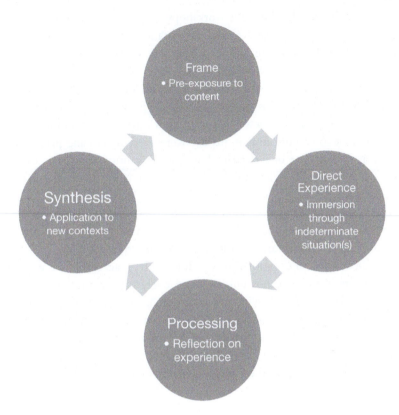

FIGURE 2.1 The learning cycle

importance placed on what Dewey termed "primary" and "secondary" experience. Primary experience is raw, empirical experience (what Kolb calls "concrete"). Secondary experience, to Dewey, is reflective experience where the experience ceases to be "isolated" and becomes integrated into greater wholes. It could be argued that many current undergraduate educational experiences lack sufficient opportunities for secondary experience. Indeed, while internship programs in higher education have grown tremendously in popularity over the last ten years, it is often the case that they are heavy on primary experience and weak on secondary experience. While students may learn a great deal when cast out on their own to complete a summer internship, for example, opportunities for a fuller integration of the experience with their undergraduate studies is often lost when Kolb's cycle stops at the "concrete" or trivializes opportunities for deeper reflection and synthesis.

27

When I lead faculty development workshops on experiential education, the biggest take-away for many is the importance of reflection in the educational process (for more on this, see Chapter 6). Clarice's experience in her internship would certainly have been much different had there not been multiple, iterative opportunities for reflection. Would she have still had "an experience"? Certainly. But this would be Dewey's "primary" experience or Kolb's "concrete" experience. Dewey was very clear on this point and noted, with caution, that some educators in his day were overemphasizing primary experience at the expense of secondary. Reading his caution today, one can see how we still struggle with this fundamental principle in experiential education.

> An experience may be immediately enjoyable and yet promote the formation of a slack and careless attitude . . . Again, experiences may be so disconnected from one another that, while each is agreeable or even exciting in itself, they are not linked cumulatively to one another. Each experience may be lively, vivid, and 'interesting,' and yet their discon- nectedness may artificially generate dispersive, disintegrated, centrifugal habits . . . They are then taken, either by way of enjoyment or of discontent and revolt, just as they come . . . Traditional education offers a plethora of examples of experiences of the kinds just mentioned.
>
> (1936, p. 26)

Isolation, disconnection, disintegration—these are real cautions today in designing student educational experience. The way to avoid creating experiences that are "interesting" yet uneducative is through careful attention to secondary experience.

So, what made Clarice's internship experience educative? Among many things, the experience was educative because it involved the purposeful elements of framing and reflection. Teachers who practice experiential education place paramount importance on these elements (we will discuss in Part 2 how to go about doing this in educationally effective ways). They structure learning opportunities that carefully frame and focus student learning, provide ample time for student-centered concrete activity and experimentation (Clarice's internship), and they purposefully design multiple and iterative stages of reflection from that primary experience. This scenario gives us a good start in describing what counts as experiential education, but, as we shall see in the following curriculum situation, this basic model does not paint a full picture of experiential education in either theory or practice.

Curriculum Situation #2: The Student Army at the University of Canterbury

Following the February 2011 earthquake in Christchurch, the University of Canterbury in New Zealand was left wondering what to do. The city center was devastated, many academic buildings were unsafe to hold classes, and yet they had thousands of students living on campus and in nearby communities who were ready to attend class. For obvious and understandable reasons, the university cancelled classes for an extended period of time following the disaster. It was anticipated that students would return home and wait for word of when the university would reopen. Something unexpected happened, however, that reveals another side of experiential education in curriculum situations.

Sam Johnson, a student at the university, realized that the earthquake and resulting devastation provided an opportunity for students to help. He went to work organizing what became known as the "UC Student Volunteer Army" (SVA) to help clean up areas of the city suffering from liquefaction—a condition where soil literally bubbles up from the ground clogging streets and sidewalks, and causing localized flooding. The soil is dense and heavy, and requires quite a bit of shoveling and tedious, backbreaking work. Sam had first started this effort in September of 2010, when the original 7.1 earthquake struck the region. What began as a simple Facebook invitation to 200 of his friends blossomed into over 2,000 volunteers organized around the city working on the clean-up (O'Steen and Perry, 2012). Following the February 2011 aftershock, which was far more devastating, the university announced an indefinite closure. But again, students responded by volunteering through the efforts of the SVA: "Over 9,000 volunteers worked 16 hours a day for over a month and utilized $1,000,000 of donated equipment and services to assist with liquefaction removal, water and hot meal distribution, assistance to the elderly and housebound, and locating missing people" (O'Steen and Perry, 2012, p. 31).

While this activity was going on, Dr. Billy O'Steen, a professor at the university and an expert on service learning, was watching a television news report on the Student Army's efforts when the broadcaster noted: "It's nice to see all of the students putting their education on hold in order to help out the Christchurch community" (p. 32). O'Steen was irked by the "putting their education on hold" comment and saw an opportunity. He contacted the university administration and proposed a service-learning course to capitalize on the students' efforts. Given the state of affairs at the university (no classes, buildings closed, etc.), O'Steen's proposal was fast-tracked and a course (Christchurch 101) was born. Over 100 students enrolled in the initial course and experienced a combination of online readings and reflections targeted on their experience in the SVA. "Looking back on it now [that first course] was pretty dirty and pretty rough," said O'Steen (2015, personal communication). But the experience showed the potential of more purposefully connecting the campus to the community far beyond simply a "one-off" course. Since that time, the course has evolved and expanded, and the University of Canterbury, somewhat surprised by the passion and energy that emerged from this student-led effort, moved quickly to capitalize on the creative momentum from the SVA. "I think it has taken a bit of time to shift people's thoughts from what they initially viewed as a pat on the back to students for shoveling silt, to viewing this as an academic endeavor," said O'Steen (2015, personal communication). UC has since established a new university-wide initiative (the Community Engagement Hub) and recognized the importance of service learning as part of the mission of the institution committing "to expand the service-learning offering to new and existing students . . . [and to make] service learning one of the four experiences of every graduate" (O'Steen and Perry, 2012, p. 32).

The university's response in creating a program around this initial effort reveals the shift we have already discussed from experiential learning to experiential education. But just as in the previous curriculum situation, we must ask ourselves *why* such an initiative might "count" as experiential education. Even with this shift, there continue to be understandable challenges at the University of Canterbury in integrating these efforts in to the academic side of the institution. The SVA case reveals differences in how one views educational activity—the volunteering efforts of the students might be laudable, some may say, but it's not *academic*. But experiential educators have long pushed back against the notion that facts alone represent the sole form of content in the educative process. To many who consider themselves experientialists, learning is a holistic endeavor—integrating the mind, body, and spirit. Curriculum, then, occurs in the midst of living, and it would only make sense to find ways to integrate "learning" and "living" through purposeful community engagement. Incorporating the "pedagogical power of place," for example, is a common curricular stance in experiential education. As Gruenewald (2003) argues:

> The point of becoming more conscious of places in education is to extend our notions of pedagogy and accountability outward toward places. Thus extended, pedagogy becomes more relevant to the lived experience of students and teachers, and accountability is re-conceptualized so that places matter to educators, students, and citizens in tangible ways.
>
> (p. 646)

From the standpoint of many, here were students and faculty who, just the day before the earthquake, may have seen little to no connection between their work in class and on campus with what was happening in their community. The earthquake provided a disruption into this routine and opened up new perspectives and thinking about the purposes and possibilities of community engagement—students who may have appeared bored, un-enthusiastic, and unmotivated in their classes and lectures were transformed into engaged, energetic, and passionate problem-solvers. Their formal classwork may have stopped after the earthquakes, but certainly their education did not (despite what the television commentator may have said). Suddenly thrust into the community, counted on to help alleviate suffering, and appreciated for their effort and their ingenuity, these students found a sense of ownership and responsibility that may have been lacking in their previous educational experience.

In addition to extending the location of learning outside the university itself, this curriculum situation reveals several other aspects of experiential education. First, students were involved in "real-world" problem solving. "Real world" is placed in quotations here because progressive educators often find the dichotomy between "school world" and "real world" to be odd. It seems to imply that what one does in school, or in the classroom, is somehow not "real." It is, of course. However, the distinction that experiential educators often make about this is one of integration—how can we integrate the school world and the world at large? Educator and founder of Outward Bound Kurt Hahn once famously quipped in his Seven Laws of Salem: "You are all crew; not passengers. Let the responsible boys and girls shoulder burdens big enough, if negligently performed, to wreck the State" (Miner 2007, p. 372). Students learn the responsibility that comes with knowledge by acting out in the democratic field of play—not while spectating from the sidelines. How do we expect students to gain the critical skills of civic engagement, of testing values against material constraints, of collaboration and consultation, if they have no such opportunities during their time at school? Hahn's notion of "crew" argues that students must do real work for them to truly understand citizenship in their communities of interest. Perhaps more provocatively, Hahn suggests that their burdens ought to matter—they ought to feel the weight of responsibility. As Art Heinricher, Dean of Undergraduate Studies at Worcester Polytechnic Institute, argues, "the problem has to be real and somebody besides the professor has to care about it" (2015, personal communication).

This leads us to another aspect of experiential education—a reconstruction of the traditional notion of "academic rigor." A taken-for-granted perspective of rigor often views it as synonymous with teacher-centered content difficulty.

If it is hard to understand initially, requires heavy instructor input, and takes a lot of work to learn (often through memorization but not always), it is "rigorous." By contrast, learning situations that are learner-centered, process-heavy, and focus on application are seen as "soft" or any of a number of other negative descriptors.[3] Rigor, of course, can mean a lot of different things. And it makes one wonder why we seem obsessed with the term given its connection to something no educator would like to see in a student—that being "rigor-mortis." Experiential educators often take the stance that one of the hardest things to do is put theory into practice. Any faculty member in a school of education can cite the oft-repeated joke about "everything I learned in my teacher education program I used in the first five minutes on my first day in the classroom. After that, I actually had to start *teaching!*" Putting theory into practice usefully is, in fact, very hard to do well.

Finally, our second curriculum situation reveals one other important aspect of experiential education—the social dimensions of learning. If we were just to take the first curriculum situation, that of the internship and the experiential learning cycle, to represent the entirety of the way we think about experiential education, we would miss significant aspects of the approach. Kolb's model is often misunderstood to locate experience and learning at the level of the individual. But, more often than not, learning and experiences are situated in social relations. As Dewey noted: "The old center was the mind . . . [t]he new center is indefinite interactions" (1929, p. 232). Many experiential curriculum projects pay particular attention to the social dimensions of learning—to these "indefinite interactions." This also happens to be supported by research in the neuroscience of learning (Bransford, 2000). In our curriculum situation here, Student Volunteer Army participants may have had individual experiences cleaning up city streets, helping city residents, or working on particular disaster relief projects, but these were not isolated or atomized. Working collaboratively in teams, and discussing and listening to each other in their service-learning course, the individual experiences become enhanced and changed through social interaction and reflection. As O'Steen recalled: "I still have students who come up to me who took that first class and tell me how much it helped them to process their experience and reflect on it with others" (2015, O'Steen personal communication).

So, what identifies the University of Canterbury case as experiential education? The purposeful connection of the campus to the community, the importance placed on authentic projects and problem solving, and the sociocultural context to learning are all hallmarks of many experiential curriculum projects. Teachers who practice experiential education look for ways to take advantage of the "pedagogical power of place"; they situate content knowledge into a broader context of learning that includes other forms of intellectual inquiry including process knowledge and holistic knowledge; and they look for ways to locate learning socially and interpersonally through collaboration and community-centered activity. Finally, they are acutely aware of how experience is "lived" and mediated within a social milieu, and not simply a chronologically isolated and individually autonomous phenomenon.

Yet this too does not cover the myriad ways experiential education is practiced. Both of our examples thus far seem to paint a picture that experiential education must, by definition, involve learning outside the classroom and campus and must be physically embodied—that is, "experiences" can only be physically situated in real time and in a particular and tangible "place." As our final curriculum situation will reveal, however, this is not always the case.

Curriculum Situation #3: The Chesapeake Bay Game at the University of Virginia

In both of the previous examples, students learned experientially by going outside (literally) the campus and classroom confines. In this sense, "learning by doing" is something that occurred while at Clarice's internship or while students participated in service in Christchurch following the earthquake. But must experiential education always involve such contexts? Are there ways we can imagine experiential environments that are not physically embodied—in other words, virtual? The answer is a resounding "yes," and this relatively unexplored area of experiential education is growing as evidenced by the rise in "virtual internships,"[4] "virtual service learning, "[5] and the "gamification" of the curriculum (Bowen 2012; Kapp, 2012). What can we learn about the theory and practice of experiential education from a virtual curriculum situation? The Chesapeake Bay Game run by the University of Virginia offers a compelling example.

In 2008, Tom Skalack, an in-coming Vice President for Research at the university challenged a group of faculty to design a large-scale simulation that modeled many of the complex socio-ecological issues surrounding the Chesapeake Bay watershed (Plank et al., 2011). Despite some initial skepticism, the interdisciplinary group came together and designed a simulation that used existing data sets (both natural and sociological) and enabled "live" role-play and interactivity within the system.

The underlying simulation model is a result of combining aggregated systems dynamics models with individual decision-making agents, both simulated and "live." These models and agents represent agriculture (some 64,000 farms), fisheries (5,000 watermen fishing for blue crab), land developers, regulators, as well as citizens residing in the watershed, a population of nearly 17 million persons. Live agents interact with the simulation model through a game "dashboard" by which they enter their decisions and review the results of played rounds.

(Plank et al., 2011, p. 4)

As might be expected, modeling as dynamic a system as a landscape scale watershed was extraordinarily complex and the group fell behind in game development. This turned out to be serendipitous, however, as it forced the faculty group to invite the student game-players to participate together rather than play remotely as originally intended (Plank 2014, personal communication). The first game was "clumsy" and numerical with no graphs or other visualizations of data. There were 100 student players who participated in the game (as key agents such as farmers, watermen, or land developers, for example). As Plank noted: "what happened in that room was really interesting to us." Rather than simply play as isolated individuals (which they were quite free to do), students began talking with each other as they experienced the consequences of their decisions in real-time on the overall socio-ecological health of the Bay. They began exchanging information, negotiating, and trying to optimize. Farmers, for example, quickly dropped high-nutrient input practices in favor of more low-yield organic practices to minimize pollution into the system. The consequences of this practical change on the economy of the region was profound, however, leading to unanticipated costs and the realization that high-yield practices, from the farmers' point of view, were quite "rational" despite the harmful downstream effects.

The UVA Bay Game has now been played by thousands of high school students, business-sector employees, and other key stakeholders in the watershed. As various participants play and replay the game, the complexity of the system reveals itself and experienced problems become discussions for possible responses and policy solutions. As one of the developers noted:

In a complex system, the results of externally applied policies may be unpredictable and even counter-productive as evidenced by unintended consequences. Seemingly rational local decisions can have adverse consequences on geographically distant actors . . . An agent-based simulation model, especially with game-like interaction, provides a platform to explore proposed policies a priori to better understand possible policy effects. No one game experience, however, will accurately 'predict' an outcome. Rather, it enables players to appreciate the complexity of the modeled environment . . . and that despite due care and consideration, unusual—emergent—outcomes may yet arise.

(Plank et al., 2011, p. 5)

According to Plank, the Bay game illustrated the pedagogical power of experiential education in several ways. First, students were immersed in a complex system. As he noted: "you can diagram a system but to be in it with others . . . that is an outcome of experiential education that is really important." The game also demands a kind of curriculum integration often not found in university settings. Rather than look at a complex socioecological system like the Chesapeake Bay from singular perspectives (environmental science, sociology, economics, etc.), the act of both creating and playing the game forced both faculty and students to take a systems perspective, including understanding at a much deeper level concepts such as nonlinear behavior, unpredictable outcomes, and adaptive management. Finally, the game stimulated innovative collaboration and interest to solve real problems both in the game and in the real world of the watershed. As players and game designers experienced setbacks, they sought new information to try to resolve problems they created in the game. The iterative process of trying to make the simulation consistent with the complex socio-ecological system of the Chesapeake Bay produced many spin-off research projects. For example, a team of faculty and students took on the challenge of infusing more graphical representations of data in the game to make the interface more user-friendly.

The UVA Bay Game as a curriculum situation brings another element to our mosaic-like exploration of experiential education and troubles some existing notions of what "counts" as educative experience. The game challenges the oft-repeated description of experiential education as "active" learning or as a "learning by doing" approach. Typically, such descriptors conjure up images of students laboring with their bodies, moving around the classroom or the community, etc. (this is certainly the case with our first two curriculum situations). Yet virtual experiences like the Bay game don't easily fit this definition. Certainly, in this case, students do not have to "go" anywhere. They can play this game from the comfort of a computer lab at the university. In addition, students are not necessarily "doing" anything particularly active—simply engaging in computer-based game play and discussing with fellow gamers. Yet it is clear that *something* about this is, in fact, experiential—the question is what?

First, to return to our previous two examples, we can see elements of our emerging understanding of experiential education at play here. The

35

components of framing, experiencing, reflecting, and synthesizing all seem to be in place in the Bay Game. Second, we can see elements of relevance, real-world problem solving, and a connection of theory to practice. Third, there is a sociality to the learning as players interact with each other and experience the benefits of collaborative inquiry. Finally, students-as-players experience the consequences of their actions in immediately pragmatic ways and, while the game itself is a simulation, they can see (and experience) the integration between their learning and the world-at-large. The Bay Game shares these pedagogical elements with our previous two examples.

Building off these intersections, the Bay Game as a curriculum situation reveals another key feature of experiential education: the role of uncertainty in the educational process. Often, educators shy away from uncertainty. The last thing we want in the classroom is confusion. The prototypical teacher in our mind is often the teacher who "turns on the lightbulb" for students, creates the "eureka!" moment, or otherwise brings order from disorder. But what if we have that all wrong? What if, rather than "aha!" moments for our students, our job is to create "huh?" moments? Scientists will tell you that some of the most profound learning takes place when the data reveals the unexpected. Dewey referred to this as the "indeterminate" situation. Experiential educators design for the indeterminate situation, the "huh?" moments. In the Bay game, no one knows how the game will turn out, creating a dynamic curriculum situation that changes as the game progresses. This is sometimes referred to as the "emergent" curriculum in the sense that the content emerges from the learning experience itself. An emergent curriculum might be contrasted, for example, with a predetermined and pre-selected curriculum where the professor (and, by extension, the students) know exactly what is to be covered and when (recall the Build-a-Bear example from Chapter 1). The notion of an emergent curriculum runs counter to the tried-and-true syllabus and linear curriculum construction many of us have been socialized into.

Blank spaces on the syllabus, unknown or ambiguous content, confusion, surprises—these are often things we wish to avoid when we plan a course. Yet experiential educators know that sometimes the most engaged learning environments are those that engender these exact states of mind. Educational anthropologist Dorothy Lee (1986) once wrote: "Are we giving up our heritage of wonder, of curiosity, of questing, of plunging into chaos and creating life out of it? Are we giving up our sense of mystery, the excitement of being lost in ambiguity and building a world out of it? Have we given up this heritage for the sake of literacy, which gives us a label instead of experience?" (p. 42). Lee's desire to create educational situations where students are excited about being "lost in ambiguity and building a world out of it" speaks directly to this key value of experiential education we have been exploring. In addition, her admonishment that we often place too much emphasis on "labels" at the expense of experience represents a fundamental characteristic of experiential approaches (we will explore the practicalities of putting experience before labels in Chapters 4 and 5). At UVA, faculty certainly could have created a course on complex systems modeling. They could have given students lots of labels (lectures) on nonlinear behavior and unpredictability. But, as Plank noted, "you can diagram a system but to be in it with others . . . that is an outcome of experiential education that is really important."

CONCLUSION

Computer simulations, virtual spaces, and other forms of "gamifying" the curriculum push against traditional notions of experiential education and also illuminate misconceptions about the approach. To "do" experiential education, one does not need to leave the classroom and the campus. One doesn't even need to have students learning "actively"—if by actively we simply mean physically active. In addition to these misconceptions, there is another I often hear during my talks and workshops with faculty—that experiential learning only really works with so-called "applied" fields. The argument here is that there are a certain number of disciplines that lend themselves easily to experiential education—fields like environmental studies, engineering, theater, sociology, education, etc. But there are other disciplines (often the traditional humanities-oriented disciplines but also some of the more "conceptual sciences" such as Math and Physics) where it is just not possible to teach "experientially." My only response here is to suggest that it is, in fact, quite possible to incorporate experiential education into any field or discipline. I have seen a Classics professor put together a wonderful active learning semester project where his students researched and implemented a public "Greek Marketplace" in conjunction with the Theater Department's performance of *Lysistrata*. I have learned about a Physics professor at Harvard, Eric Mazur, who runs an introductory Physics course experientially through a peer instruction model (for more on Eric Mazur, see Chapter 3). The Reacting To The Past curriculum[6] demonstrates how history concepts and examples can be made far more experiential than we see in a typical college classroom. And the "public humanities" model demonstrated by Brown alongside the community-based research work at many universities including Princeton[7] reveal that there is simply no limit to experiential pedagogy *across* the liberal arts except for our own imaginations.

As I hope each of our curriculum situations have revealed, experiential education comes in many forms and is not easily codified into a single methodology or teaching technique. However, by focusing on the commonalities that appear in various curriculum situations, we can elucidate what is most often valued in experiential education. Our three curriculum situations reveal many of those commonalities:

- The crucial components of the experiential learning "cycle" including framing, concrete experience, reflection, and synthesis.
- The pragmatic approach that connects the curriculum to real-world problem solving.
- The importance of designing for the "indeterminate situation" in learning.
- The high degree of student ownership and co-constructed learning at play.

I have not attempted here to categorically state what experiential education "is" in all times and contexts. But that does not mean that anything can count as experiential education. There are, in fact, common practices for the approach. And while the methodologies employed are quite varied, as we shall see in Chapter 3, the pedagogy is reasonably well defined and understood. Returning to our notion of experiential education as a "social language," the language structure is the same even as the dialect changes. Spanish, Italian, French, and Portuguese, for example, share a common language origin with "Vulgar Latin." To the untrained eye (and ear), these languages may at first appear to have nothing in common with one another. But once you begin to see the structures they share in common, patterns of understanding emerge. Approaches such as problem-based learning, community-based learning, active learning, and integrative learning may not, at first, appear to share much in common, but once you know what to look for, you can see how they all connect through a common structure—that of experiential education. And that structure is what I point to when someone asks what "counts" as experiential education.

NOTES

1. I use the word "basic" here intentionally. In many respects, the first three chapters of this book are an attempt to define experiential education and this definition should not be seen as the final word on the subject.
2. The student's name has been changed.

3. It is not too difficult to take a feminist perspective on this debate as well—where "soft" is equated to academic endeavors that are relational, embedded, and holistic whereas "hard" academic endeavors are individualistic, context free, and highly competitive.
4. See "An Internship From Your Couch": http://online.wsj.com/news/articles/SB10001424052748704471504574441132945681314?mg=reno64-
5. See Maxine, Sable, and Cristiano (2010). "Service Learning and Virtual Worlds."
6. For more information, see the RTTP website: https://reacting.barnard.edu/
7. For more on the Brown University Public Humanities program, see: www.brown.edu/academics/public-humanities/. For information about Princeton's Community Based Learning Initiative see: www.princeton.edu/cbli/

REFERENCES

Association for Experiential Education (AEE). Retrieved June 18, 2014 from: www.aee.org/about/what-is-ee

Bowen, J. A. (2012). *Teaching Naked: How Moving Technology out of your College Classroom will Improve Student Learning*. San Francisco, CA: Jossey Bass.

Bransford, J. (2000). *How People Learn: Brain, Mind, Experience, and School*. Washington, DC: National Academies Press.

Dewey, J. (1938). *Experience and Education*. New York: Collier Macmillan.

Dewey, J. ([1929] 1981). *The Later Works, 1925–1953: 1925*. Carbondale, IL: Southern Illinois University.

Gadamer, H. G., & Dutt, C. (2001). *Gadamer in Conversation: Reflections and Commentary*. New Haven, CT and London: Yale University Press.

Greene, M. (1988). *The Dialectic of Freedom*. New York: Teachers College Press.

Gruenewald, D. A. (2003). Foundations of place: A multidisciplinary framework for place-conscious education. *American Educational Research Journal, 40*(3), 619–654.

Heinricher, A. (2015). Personal communication.

Itin, C. M. (1999). Reasserting the philosophy of experiential education as a vehicle for change in the 21st century. *Journal of Experiential Education, 22*(2), 91–98.

James, W. (1907). *Pragmatism, A New Name for Some Old Ways of Thinking: Popular Lectures on Philosophy*. New York: Longmans, Green.

Jay, M. (2005). *Songs of Experience: Modern American and European Variations on a Universal Theme*. Berkeley, CA: University of California Press.

Jensen, E. (2005). *Teaching with the Brain in Mind* (2nd ed.). Alexandria, VA: Association for Supervision and Curriculum Development.

Joplin, L. (2008). On defining experiential education. In K. Warren, D. Mitten, & T. A. Loeffler (Eds.), *The Theory and Practice of Experiential Education* (pp. 16–23). Boulder, CO: Association for Experiential Education.

Kapp, K. M. (2012). *The Gamification of Learning and Instruction: Game-based Methods and Strategies for Training and Education*. New York: John Wiley & Sons.

Kolb, D. A. (1984). *Experiential Learning: Experience as the Source of Learning and Development*. Upper Saddle, NJ: Prentice-Hall.

Lee, D. (1986). *Valuing the Self: What we can Learn from Other Cultures*. Prospect Heights, IL: Waveland Press.

Maxim, B., Matthew Sable, & John Cristiano (2010). *Service Learning and Virtual Worlds*. Proceedings from the 40th ASEE/IEEE Frontiers in Education Conference.

Miner, J. L. (2002). *Outward Bound USA: Crew not Passengers*. Seattle, WA: Mountaineers Books.

Oakeshott, M. (1933). *Experience and its Modes*. London: Cambridge University Press.

O'Steen, B. (2015). Personal communication.

O'Steen, B., & Perry, L. (2012). Born from the rubble: The origins of service-learning in New Zealand and an expansion of the diffusion of innovation curve. *Jefferson Journal of Science and Culture*, 2, pp. 27–34.

Plank, J. (2014). Personal communication.

Plank, J., Feldon, D., Sherman, W., & Elliot, J. (2011). Complex systems, interdisciplinary collaboration, and institutional renewal. *Change: The Magazine of Higher Learning*, 43(3), pp. 35–43.

Roberts, J. W. (2012). *Beyond Learning by Doing: Theoretical Currents in Experiential Education*. New York: Routledge.

Seaman, J. (2014). Personal communication.

Chapter 3

Models and Methodologies of Experiential Education

I am large, I contain multitudes

(Walt Whitman, "Song of Myself," from *Leaves of Grass*, 1855)

INTRODUCTION

There is an incredible array of terminology used in higher education to describe experiential approaches. A survey of the literature reveals the following commonly used terms (sorted alphabetically) that evoke or connect in some way to experiential education:

- Active learning
- Adult learning
- Adventure education
- Authentic learning
- Career and technical education
- Challenge education
- Civic engagement
- Collaborative learning
- Community-based learning
- Cooperative learning
- Democratic education
- Education for sustainability
- Environmental education
- Game-based learning
- Hands-on learning
- Holistic education

- Integrated learning
- Inquiry-based learning
- Outdoor education
- Place-based education
- Problem-based learning
- Project-based learning
- Service learning
- Transformative learning
- Vocational education
- Work-integrated learning

How could curricular approaches as varied as "adventure education," "cooperative learning," "service learning," and "vocational education" be considered the same thing? It is clear that there is quite a haze around experiential education as used in the literature. And, while there have been a few attempts to map the discourse per se, more descriptors and terms appear seemingly overnight as college and university marketing departments scramble for the latest distinctive pedagogical promised land. There is no clear organizational structure, no hierarchy or nomenclature of terms that is generally agreed upon. This is not unusual when a field is relatively young. While experiential education certainly goes back to the early 1900s in terms of its use in higher education (the University of Cincinnati, for example, started the first Cooperative Education program in 1906), the last 30–40 years have witnessed a dramatic rise in its use. A Google "Ngram Reader" search which tracks the frequency of a given term in books over time is revealing. The chart below tracks the frequency of the term "experiential education" from 1800 to 2008.[1]

As one can see, while there was a brief and small spike signaled by the Progressive Education Era of the early 1900s, the term dramatically increased in frequency in the late 1960s and has continued to rise through to 2008. Because of the fields' relative "youth," a consensus typology has yet to be settled upon. This, of course, is both advantageous and a challenge for both proponents and practitioners. As Saltmarsh et al. describe (2009):

[t]his lack of clarity has the very real advantage of enabling a broad range of people to feel they are part of the movement. Vague language, however, also runs the risk of portraying a movement that stands for anything and therefore nothing. Can we find a language that has wide 'traction' but also inspires?

(p. 4)

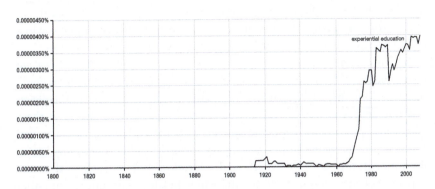

FIGURE 3.1 Google Ngram of "experiential education"

So while it is clear that the current conversation about experiential education in higher education is quite muddled, it is nonetheless important to seek some degree of common language in order to both gain traction and inspire, as Saltmarsh et al. argue above. I believe that experiential education can be a unifying term—one that has the potential to mean something (rather than anything) and, potentially, to inspire faculty and administrators in higher education to consider its educative and transformative potential. In what follows, I will attempt to map the terminology and nomenclature, not as some final answer to a still-growing and changing field, but rather to work toward some better degree of clarity without falling victim to definitional purity. Mooney and Edwards (2001), in their own typology on community-based learning (CBL), importantly noted:

> We want to avoid two common pitfalls: the reification of the typology itself, and the mirage that definitional consensus is a prerequisite of improved praxis. Typologies ... are useful deductive propositions that enable investigators and practitioners alike to make provisional sense out of the complex social realities represented by the increased popularity of CBL in higher education. Yet, typologies of this sort often become counter-productive. If pushed beyond their heuristic limits, they foster definitional disputes about what fits which type and to what extent. Such 'boundary maintenance' efforts lead to ever more fine-grained description, but not to ever-improving praxis.
>
> (p. 190)

Like Edwards and Mooney, I am not too concerned about achieving conceptual consensus and I don't necessarily see this as a weakness that must

43

somehow be "fixed" before we can proceed with practice. It would be ironic indeed, for proponents of experiential education, to lose sight of praxis while following abstracted definitional mirages. We can, in fact, learn by doing.

In this chapter, we will explore a variety of pedagogical models that are often linked to experiential education in an attempt to organize an "ecosystem" of sorts. Along the way, we will use illustrative examples from various colleges and universities as well as faculty practitioners to demonstrate how these approaches play out in real contexts. I have attempted here to use cases that I believe are particularly noteworthy in terms of either a teaching or an institutional approach to experiential education, not to suggest that any experiential attempt must replicate these individuals or institutions but rather to give a sense of what these models look like in practice. In the Appendix, I have included a list of institutional examples by type for further reference.

THE ECOSYSTEM OF EXPERIENTIAL EDUCATION

If experiential education is not simply a method to be used by a teacher in an instructional moment, what is it? Itin (1999) argues that, properly understood, experiential education is a philosophy. He states:

> if experiential education is correctly identified as a philosophy, it allows for the various expressions of this philosophy (service learning, cooperative learning, adventure-based, problem-based, action learning, etc.) to be linked together under this single philosophy. This provides a method for bringing those together who promote these various expressions and to argue for educational reform that would support experiential education in all settings.
>
> (p. 97)

While I take some issue with framing experiential education as a philosophy,[2] Itin has made a useful move here. Framing experiential education this way avoids the vulnerabilities of equating it with an informal process or isolated method (experiential learning), while at the same time allowing for a number of curricular projects and pedagogical approaches to find a coherent home underneath the broader and systematic process (experiential education). Extending from Itin, we might think of experiential education as an ecosystem of sorts. In biology, an ecosystem is a community of interacting components (typically defined as organisms and the physical environment). Meadows (2008) defines a system as "a set of things—people, cells, molecules, or whatever—interconnected in such a way that they produce their own pattern of behavior over time" (p. 2). In this sense, there are a variety of pedagogical approaches and curricular models that are interconnected such that they have produced their own "system"—in this case a pedagogical system we know as "experiential education." Each component piece may have its own character (and possibly even subsystem), but it is connected to other components through the commonality of the pedagogy and it is that interconnection that defines the system as a whole. Experiential education, as opposed to experiential learning, is an ecosystem of pedagogical processes held together through commonalities with each other. In what follows, I briefly explore this ecosystem, noting what I consider to be the most prominent (though certainly not all) of the component pieces seen in higher education.

A NOMENCLATURE OF EXPERIENTIAL EDUCATION

If experiential education is the pedagogical common denominator, it sits at the center of the system (not unlike the sun in our solar system). Orbiting around this center are several broad conceptual categories: active learning, community-based learning, integrative learning, and project-based learning. Each of these categories has within it a variety of specific experiential method-ologies such as service projects, internships, simulations, and case studies. While each may represent highly varied approaches, they are defined as a system in the sense that they are all defined by their relationship with the central pedagogical core—experiential education.

A careful reader will notice that I have labeled each of these conceptual categories with the term "learning" to continue to emphasize that these more methodological approaches fit into a broader and more systematic process of teaching and learning. However, it is worth noting that some may take issue with this organizational structure. What about "service learning," "cooperative learning," and "place-based learning," for example? I have elected to place these approaches underneath broader categories (such as "community-based" learning in the case of service learning and "active learning" in the case of cooperative learning). What about other approaches typically associated with experiential education such as outdoor education and environmental education? In these cases, I think an argument can be made that they stand on their own in terms of the distinct content associated with their processes (notice again that I have labeled each of these with the term "education" as opposed to learning). But isn't community-based learning its own educational and systematic approach, for example, irrespective of experiential education? A reasonable argument can be made that many of these subcategories of experiential education could, in fact, stand on their own as broader educational approaches. But it is also the case that each of them draws from experiential

45

FIGURE 3.2 Ecosystem of "experiential education"

education in terms of how they organize the process of teaching and learning. To return to our example of community-based learning, it is not just the "community" element that makes the activity educational, it is the purposeful framing and reflection on that experience that makes it so. It is this central teaching and learning *process* that draws from the larger ideas of experiential education. To be sure, there is some overlap with these and, as such, the categories and organization of the terms themselves will always be blurred and somewhat arbitrary.[3] Nonetheless, some attempt to organize the landscape is important in order to discuss the ways experiential education is both "done" and talked about on college campuses and it is for this reason that it is worth a brief tour of the landscape. In what follows, I will discuss each of these four major conceptual categories of experiential education in turn: active learning, community-based learning, integrative learning, and project-based learning.

Active Learning

Active learning is an umbrella term for a range of instructional strategies aimed at increasing student involvement and ownership of their learning. Early discussions of active learning often framed it as techniques or initiatives that a teacher can do in the classroom to liven up more "passive" forms of teaching and learning that comes with lecturing (Bonwell and Eisen, 1991). Techniques such as think–pair shares, Socratic questioning, writing prompts, debates, role-plays, and peer-to-peer teaching are all staples of active learning teaching strategies. For example, Bowen (2012) notes:

> [t]he term *active learning* includes a wide range of pedagogies from class writing and discussion to role playing and lab work as well as collaborative, cooperative, and problem-based learning. Many of these labels and techniques overlap: all collaborative learning is done in a group, but it is also almost always active learning.
>
> (p. 192, emphasis in text)

Here again we see the confusion of nomenclature evident in experiential education more broadly. Precise definitions of active learning (and as we have been discussing, experiential education), are hard to come by. Nonetheless, there are some commonalities to the approach. As Bonwell and Eison noted:

> Though the term "active learning" has never been precisely defined in the educational literature, some general characteristics are commonly associated with the use of strategies promoting active learning in the classroom: students are involved more than listening; less emphasis is placed on transmitting information and more on developing students' skills; students are involved in higher-order thinking; students are engaged in activities; and, greater emphasis is placed on student's exploration of their own attitudes and values.
>
> (p. 2)

A Google Ngram Reader[4] search of the term indicates its growing prominence in the literature.

Part of the reason for this increase comes from evidence-based support of its usage in what has been described as the "new science of learning" literature

47

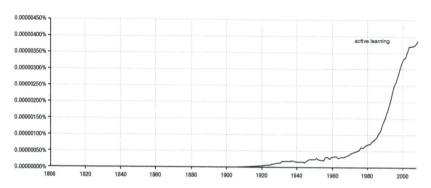

FIGURE 3.3 Google Ngram of "active learning"

(Ambrose et al., 2010; Bransford et al., 2000; Pelligrino and Hilton, 2012). It is clear from this research, for example, that the human brain is far more "plastic" and interactive than we previously understood. As Caine and Caine (1991) noted: "We know that the learning brain is an active brain" (p. 156). Helping students "own" their learning and actively process their experiences has been shown to be an important factor in increasing the transfer of learning to new contexts and domains—what has been typically labeled as "metacognition" (Bransford et al., 2000). And Bowen (2012) argues:

> [w]hile the classroom seems an ideal place for challenging and exploring new ideas, furiously transcribing oral content is clearly not the ideal learning activity for teaching critical thinking. Active learning has been demonstrated to improve retention of content but it can also stimulate critical thinking.
>
> (p. 196)

Another reason for the increased prominence of active learning in the higher education literature is the increased attention to technology and "flipped classrooms." As innovations in Web-based interfaces continue to make in-roads into the traditional college lecture-based classroom, pressure mounts for the value proposition of a bricks and mortar campus. Active learning potentially provides one rationale for what a teacher can do differently or more effectively face-to-face than they can in a "distance learning" environment.

Thus, while active learning also does not necessarily have to involve physical activity, more often than not an active learning educational space involves both the mind and the body (even if that just means getting up off your chair and joining a discussion group). This does make one to wonder, however, how or why "active" learning can only happen face-to-face. As our UVA Bay Game example reveals in Chapter 2, this is not necessarily the case. The University of Minnesota Active Learning Classrooms initiative, for example, provides a compelling example of how face-to-face active learning and technology can be conjoined and not seen as oppositional (for more information, see the Appendix). Nevertheless, the dominant discourse in higher education around active learning and experiential education seems to position it as an "in-person" approach. Whether face-to-face or not, active learning is seen as a core methodology of experiential education because of its heavy emphasis on learner-centric knowledge creation. The Association for Experiential Education, for example, discusses one of the principles of the approach this way: "the learner is actively engaged in posing questions, investigating, experimenting, being curious, solving problems, assuming responsibility, being creative, and constructing meaning"(AEE, no date). It is important to re-emphasize here that active learning and experiential education are not synonymous. Active learning can be employed as a technique or method in a variety of classroom contexts. While it is almost always present as part of the broader processes of experiential education, the broader processes of experiential education are not always present in active learning.

Faculty Case Example of Active Learning: Eric Mazur, Physics, Harvard University

Eric Mazur currently holds the chair of the Balkanski Professor of Physics and Applied Physics at Harvard. Dr. Mazur utilizes an instructional strategy he refers to as "Peer Instruction" or "PI" and has written a book on the subject (*Peer Instruction: A User's Manual*, 1997). In *Peer Instruction*, students are given open-ended prompts—what Mazur labels "ConcepTests" in between periods of direct instruction. Students first work on these questions individually and then in small groups of three–four attempting to reach consensus on an answer. This particular approach to active learning peer instruction has been studied and found to be more beneficial than either lecturing or whole class discussion (Monterola, Roxes, and Carreon-Monterola, 2009). Mazur notes that he teaches one of the two semester introduction to Physics courses in this way and that "he will never go back" (personal communication, 2015).

Institutional Case Example of Active Learning: Brevard College

Brevard College, a small liberal arts school in western North Carolina, serves as a useful case study in terms of what an institutional focus on "active learning" looks like on a college or university campus. In 2009, the institution used a mandated accreditation process to create a Quality Enhancement Plan (QEP) to focus on student engagement with an emphasis on "Pedagogies for Engaged and Actively-Learning Students" (Bringle, Kafsky, and Keiser, 2015, personal communication). The college developed a systematic faculty development program to support faculty's implementation of active learning through thematic teaching circles, teaching dyads, and mini-grants for fieldwork to enhance classroom instruction. Teaching Circles and Dyads provide faculty with a chance to converse and enact experiential methods to promote critical thinking and reflection in their individual classes. For example, the Business and Organizational Leadership Department applied for funds to sustain a curricular review and redesign of their large introductory courses to focus on more experiential methods. As Keiser notes:

> teaching grants allow faculty to make their creative, engaging teaching a reality. For example, rather than just learn about nutrition, Health Science majors plan, prepare, and partake in a healthy Thanksgiving meal. Rather than just learn about religions from a textbook, students participate in a Houses of Worship tour, meeting face to face with believers of different faiths.
>
> (2015, personal communication)

In 2014, Brevard College's Faculty and Board decided to revise the college's mission statement to center on "experiential learning" as an outcome born from the initial effort to engage student learners and empower active learning. The College's succinct mission statement now states: "Brevard College is committed to an experiential liberal arts education that encourages personal growth and inspires artistic, intellectual, and social action" (Brevard College, no date). A shared definition of experiential education is now promoted on every syllabus creating a shared culture of experiential education among the faculty. The work is on-going, however. Keiser notes that

> as the college moves into the next phase of implementation, it will be critical that faculty have access to resources to deepen their understanding of experiential education. Faculty want help to plan meaningful learning experiences that offer authentic opportunities for students to grapple with course content. However, extracting learning after these purposeful learning moments is dependent often on the facilitation skills of the professor to guide their students' reflection.
>
> (2015, personal communication)

Community-based Learning

While community-based learning (CBL) has been an increasingly popular and utilized approach in higher education, it is not a new phenomenon. Volunteering and other forms of community engagement have been around since the early days of the Progressive Era when educators sought to connect school with real world settings. Beyond these early attempts, theoretical work by Paulo Freire (1970), Daloz et al. (1996), Ernest Boyer (1997), David Orr (2002), and many others argue that the university should be more responsive to community needs and that the intellectual life (and thus faculty scholarship) should be more intimately tied to ideas of "praxis" and social change. Richard Rorty (1998) argued that the academy had become "spectatorial and retrospective" (p. 14) and needed to be more intimately connected to societal concerns. While CBL is not new per se, it is also worth noting that the last several decades have witnessed a dramatic increase in the total number and variety of CBL projects and programs in higher education. Looking again at the Google Ngram Reader, the term "community-based learning" doesn't appear in books prior to 1965. It spikes up dramatically between 1965 and 1980 and then again into 2008 when the data capture stops.[5]

There are a variety of reasons for the increased interest in CBL. From the pragmatic—colleges and universities are realizing the educative potential in experiential engagement beyond campus—to the skeptical, such programs fit nicely into efficiency and neoliberal narratives of education as "workforce development," CBL is unquestionably on the rise. But, just as with active learning, there is difficulty in finding a precise definition and the approach can easily become a catch-all for a variety of initiatives. As Mooney and Edwards (2001) argue:

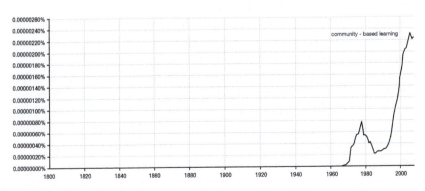

FIGURE 3.4 Google Ngram of "community-based learning"

For those who have the occasion to develop or oversee a variety of CBL options, the differences between internships, experiential learning, volunteering, cocurricular community service, preprofessional experiences, practica, co-ops, community service, and applied learning may seem to be relatively clear-cut. However, among faculty members and administrators considering the full range of CBL endeavors for the first time, such distinctions may not be obvious.

(p. 184)

As Mooney and Edwards aptly demonstrate, the conceptual haze that surrounds CBL (and, again, experiential education more broadly) is substantial. Nonetheless, just as with active learning, there is some degree of commonly understood practice. Saltmarsh, Hartley, and Clayton (2009) offer a basic definition of what they term "civic engagement" that, in my view, is synonymous with CBL: "some kind of activity (a course, a research project, internships, fieldwork, clinical placement, economic development, volunteerism) that occurs in the 'community' (local, national, global). The focus on place often leads to the work of engagement being labeled 'community engagement,' or activity that occurs in a certain place—'the community'" (p. 6).

There are a variety of approaches that fit underneath the CBL umbrella, including place-based learning, service learning, and community-based research to name some of the most prominent forms in higher education. CBL is typically seen as a core methodology within experiential education because of its emphasis on connecting the "school world" and the "real world"—an important stance of progressive educators from John Dewey, Jane Addams, and Rudolph Steiner up to proponents of critical pedagogy such as Paulo Freire, Maxine Greene, and Peter McLaren. A key distinguishing characteristic of the approach is its emphasis on off-campus activity. CBL, almost by definition, takes place away from campus boundaries and outside the classroom walls (whereas active learning and the other methods explored in this chapter do not necessarily have to). As Saltmarsh et al. (2009) state: "However, mere activity in the community does not comprise an educative endeavor. And, in fact, there is more than a little concern that community-based activity, not properly framed, is *worse* than no engagement at all" (p. 4). Poorly run service trips that objectify marginalized communities and reinforce stereotypes along with university-initiated programs to "save" the local community all have the potential to do real damage and miseducate rather than build capacity in both students and community partners alike. The emerging field of "critical service learning" has a lot to say about such approaches. Here again, CBL is not synonymous with experiential education. While CBL is often utilized in experiential education, not all CBL activities employ the broader processes of experiential education. Though I think it probably is true that effective CBL almost always draws from the broader processes and design frameworks of experiential education (for more about these practical specifics, see Chapters 4–6).

Faculty Case Example of Community-based Learning

The senior capstone experience for students majoring in Environmental Studies at Earlham College involves an "Integrated Research Project" or IRP. The IRP is a project-based research initiative developed in conjunction with the city of Richmond. Each year, the teaching faculty member responsible for the capstone works with staff from the Center for Integrated Learning to "curate" a list of research needs from the city that have environmental themes. Students then choose a research project that involves a combination of academic background research and community-based "applied" research and activity. Research projects in the past have included developing an online map of the city and its sustainability-related assets, a feasibility study for an expanded downtown farmers market, and an evaluation of a grant-funded neighborhood blight elimination project. Results of the research were presented to city officials at the conclusion of the project along with a public presentation of the results.

Institutional Case Example of Community-based Learning: Siena College

Siena College in Loudonville, New York, serves as an excellent case study for what can happen when an institution commits to integrating community-based learning in deep and pervasive ways. Beginning with a small staff organized around a fledgling AmeriCorps VISTA fellows program, Siena's Center for "Academic Community Engagement" (ACE) has grown to 14 staff, over 200 student undergraduate participants, and 34 postgraduates. Directed by a member of the teaching faculty (Matthew Johnson, Associate Professor of Sociology and Environmental Studies), ACE comprises nine separate programs targeted toward giving students experiential opportunities to engage in community-based learning. Each program is branded to reach a different student demographic and meet a specific community need. Programs include "Community Corps" which combines community volunteering with a summer internship, "Next" where students act as consultants for local non-profits and businesses, and "Community Engaged Teaching and Learning" which works with teaching faculty and disciplinary departments to integrate community-based learning into existing academic courses and curricula.

According to Johnson:"Each of ACE's programs weaves together long-term, intensive engagement with community partners within the framework of a three-year partnership plan between the college and the partner. This includes a developmental pathway culminating in leadership of a team or teams of students in each site, an academic certificate degree pathway, and intensive professional development and mentoring throughout the program" (2015, personal communication).

Integrative Learning

The term "du jour" at the time of this writing appears to be "Integrative Learning" as highlighted by recent AACU publications and conferences around that theme.[6] One recent article claims that integrative learning "may one day take its rightful place alongside breadth and depth as a hallmark of a quality undergraduate education" (Huber, Hutchens, and Gale 2005, p. 4). Returning again to our issue of hazy terms, "integrative learning" seems to take the problem to its logical conclusion by signaling something so vague and diffuse that hardly anyone would be against it. As a test of whether something is platitudinous, consider whether anyone would ever be for its conceptual opposite. Who would claim to be a champion for "disintegrated learning" after all? Nonetheless, the vagueness of integrative learning is also its strength. As colleges and universities look to capitalize on a more comprehensive and holistic sense of a students' experience, "integrative learning" provides an effective conceptual home for a range of approaches and initiatives. And, while relatively new to the scene, there is already some clarity emerging about what it is. The AAC&U, in partnership with the Carnegie Foundation, released "A Statement on Integrative Learning" in 2004 that described the approach in the following way:

> Integrative learning comes in many varieties: connecting skills and knowledge from multiple sources and experiences; applying theory to practice in various settings; utilizing diverse and even contradictory points of view; and, understanding issues and positions contextually. Significant knowledge within individual disciplines serves as the foundation, but integrative learning goes beyond traditional academic boundaries. Indeed, integrative experiences often occur as learners address real-world problems, unscripted and sufficiently broad to require multiple areas of knowledge

and multiple modes of inquiry, offering multiple solutions and benefiting from multiple perspectives.

(p. 13)

While it may be true that much of what is listed here describes what we already know to be effective in terms of liberal education, it is the intentionality of integrative learning approaches that makes the difference. As Huber, Hutchins, and Gale (2005) note: "the capacity for integrative learning—for connection making—has come to be recognized as an important learning outcome in its own right, not simply a hoped-for consequence of the mix of experiences that constitute undergraduate education" (p. 5). The Google Ngram viewer of the term demonstrates its increased popularity and reveals a similar pattern to our other core methodologies with a beginning around the progressive era and a precipitous rise beginning in the 1990s to 2008.[7]

One of the most prominent (and rapidly expanding) approaches within this conceptual category in higher education are work-integration projects and initiatives. The reasons for this are easy to see. As colleges and universities attempt to respond to the post-2008 global recession, the need for a more robust integration of career education with the academic curriculum has become mission critical. The old paradigm of a small "career services" office tucked away in some forgotten corner of the campus has been replaced by a new image of career development that is deep, pervasive, and integrated throughout a student's four-year career. Internships, externships, newly formulated work-study experiences, and alumni-student mentorships have been hallmarks of this new approach.

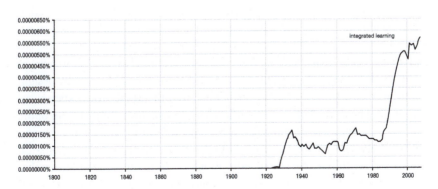

FIGURE 3.5 Google Ngram of "integrated learning"

In a report entitled "A Roadmap for Transforming the College-to-Career Experience," edited by Andy Chan and Tommy Derry of Wake Forest University, Chan (2013) argues:

> While transformational changes have occurred in the world of work, many college career offices look and function the same way they did twenty years ago. When we think about how dramatically the world of work has changed, it is remarkable that the methods utilized to prepare students to enter it have remained static . . . Unless we can demonstrate to prospective students and their families that the four years spent at college will result in better employment prospects, there will continue to be those who disparage a college education as a waste of money . . . In order to seriously affect systemic change, there must be institutional prioritization, including senior administration and faculty commitment, as well as partnerships between the career office and influential groups around campus, particularly academic, advancement, communications, information systems and alumni relations offices.
>
> (p. 2)

While integrative learning refers to the variety of ways we can connect student experience and learning, it is clear that integrating "curriculum to career" is a clear driver in this area and is dramatically changing the landscape of higher education across all sectors. Chan, in another context, even went so far as to say "career services must die"[8] in the sense that the old, disintegrated model for career support must be replaced by a more developmental, purposeful, and integrated approach.

Integrative learning is a significant conceptual category of experiential education because of the ways in which it seeks to overtly make connections between and among student experiences. Whether that is through connecting work experiences with the academic curriculum, integrating across various academic domains and intellectual ways of knowing, or integrating in-class and out-of-class experiences more broadly. Central to this approach, as mentioned above, is intentionality. Learning experiences have to be by design, not by accident. And the design principles draw, at their core, from experiential education. The critical importance of orchestrating appropriate framing of the educative experience, of guided inquiry and reflection, and of meaningful linkages between various experiences all draw from the common pedagogical approaches within experiential education. In fact, one might argue that without meaningful orchestration of experience, integrative learning is not even possible—except haphazardly and with "chance" encounters such as when a student has an "aha" moment in class when concepts or topics introduced connect to something she has learned in another context. This does, in fact, already happen from time to time on college campuses but the point is that it will happen more regularly and more effectively if it is planned for and intentionally designed into the learning experience. And, in fact, we are seeing significant movement on college and university campuses to set up administrative structures to enable this intentionality.[9]

Faculty Case Example of Integrative Learning: Elly Vandergrift, University of Oregon

Elly Vandergrift, Science Literacy Program Associate Director at the University of Oregon, co-designed a team-taught integrated course on "bread" along with three biologists, a physicist, and a professor of English. The course was part of the honors college at Oregon and was funded in part from a Howard Hughes Medical Institute grant to improve general education in the sciences. Students (juniors and senior non-science majors) learned about bread from multiple disciplines, created their own sourdough starters, took field trips to local bakeries and a mill, and met with topical experts including a local food writer and a food geneticist. Vandergrift noted: "we wanted an integrative experience that went across the entire term" (personal communication, 2015). The course combined interdisciplinary team teaching, community engagement, and real-world experimentation as students had several integrative science-based research assignments connected to bread-making and production. To Vandergrift, the point of the course design was to "create a science course that would really resonate with students." In the post-course evaluations, students noted that the integrated design allowed the course content to be more engaging and relevant overall.

Institutional Case Example of Integrative Learning: Northeastern University

Northeastern University's Cooperative Education program (co-op) is nationally renowned for their work-integrated learning model combining traditional academic study with long-term immersion for up to six months in the workplace. Much more than a traditional internship, the NU Co-op model has been in operation for over 100 years and includes purposeful integration of the work experience into a student's academic career by alternating semesters of academic study with semesters of full-time employment (up to two co-ops are possible on a four-year plan and up to three on a five-year plan according to the university's website: www.northeastern.edu/coop/ students/overview/).

Students undergo a co-op orientation prior to their experience, are assigned a co-op advisor, and are asked to integrate their learning on their co-op back into their academic studies in a variety of ways. "We define experiential education as the ability to combine theory and practice and really gain deep learning," says Susan Ambrose, Senior Vice Provost of undergraduate education and experiential learning at Northeastern. "What we believe is the strength of the co-op is that you don't have to approximate the real world because you are situating students in it" (personal communication, 2014). The majority of students (approximately 70 percent) do two or more co-ops during their time at NU and the experiences are usually six months in length. Both domestic and international co-op experiences are available for students. The advantages of such an approach in terms of undergraduate career preparation and readiness are tremendous. As Maria Stein, Associate Vice President of Cooperative Education and Career Development, noted: "with all the debate we hear now about the skills gap and employers not being able to find the right mix of skills and talent that they need, a co-op program such as ours enables employers to work with us to deliver those skills . . . and our students are learning early on what it means to be a professional" (personal communication, 2014).

Problem and Project-based Learning

The last core methodology in the experiential education ecosystem is "project-based learning" (PBL). And, just as with the other methodologies explored in this chapter, there are a variety of ways this approach is described. "Inquiry-based," "problem-based," "project-based," and "discovery-based" have all, at some point, been used to describe the basics of this experiential method. Duch, Groh, and Allen (2001), for example, use the term "problem-based learning" and describe the approach this way:

> In the problem-based approach, complex, real-world problems are used to motivate students to identify and research the concepts and principles they need to know to work through those problems. Students work in small learning teams, bringing together collective skill at acquiring, communicating, and integrating information.
>
> (p. 6)

Hmelo-Silver, Duncan, and Chinn (2007), on the other hand, view problem-based learning and inquiry-based learning (IL) as distinct but also pedagogically connected. They argue:

In PBL students learn content, strategies, and self-directed learning skills through collaboratively solving problems, reflecting on their experiences, and engaging in self-directed inquiry. In IL, students learn content as well as discipline specific reasoning skills and practices (often in scientific disciplines) by collaboratively engaging in investigations.

(p. 100)

Inquiry-based learning appears to be used most often in the sciences while problem-based learning is used in other fields and disciplines. Finally, a recent blog post by Larmer (2014) in Edutopia describes the various approaches this way:

We decided to call problem-based learning a subset of project-based learning—that is, one of the ways a teacher could frame a project is "to solve a problem."

Problem-based learning typically follow prescribed steps:

1. Presentation of an "ill-structured" (open-ended, "messy") problem;
2. Problem definition or formulation (the problem statement);
3. Generation of a "knowledge inventory" (a list of "what we know about the problem" and "what we need to know");
4. Generation of possible solutions;
5. Formulation of learning issues for self-directed and coached learning;
6. Sharing of findings and solutions.

If you're a project-BL teacher, this probably looks pretty familiar, even though the process goes by different names. Other than the framing and the more formalized steps in problem-BL, there's really not much conceptual difference between the two PBLs—it's more a question of style and scope.

I think Larmer frames the issue well here. "PBL," whether described as "project-BL" or "problem-BL," is essentially the same pedagogical approach with the possible difference being that problems can be (but are not always) shorter and more narrowly framed than projects. You could imagine, for example, a problem-based learning initiative that covers only a single class period but it is hard to envision a project-based learning initiative so structured. In any case, all the various forms draw from the same pedagogical "taproot" of experiential education, and, for the purposes here, I have chosen to organize them under the core methodology of "Project-based learning" (PBL).

PBL is a significant conceptual category of experiential education for a number of reasons. First, the design of the educative experience around a "messy" problem or otherwise loosely structured issue is a fundamental

59

component of experiential design. The definition of experiential education offered by the Association of Experiential Education discussed earlier describes the role of the learner and the teachers such that "[t]he educator and learner may experience success, failure, adventure, risk-taking and uncertainty, because the outcomes of experience cannot totally be predicted" (AEE, no date). This uncertainty comes from the intentionally open-ended design of both PBL and experiential education. PBL also draws from experiential education in its focus on relevant, real-life issues or events. Sometimes framed by the instructor and sometimes by the students themselves, these projects or problems help organize "just-in-time" learning and authentic assessment. Again, according to the AEE definition of experiential education: "Throughout the experiential learning process, the learner is actively engaged in posing questions, investigating, experimenting, being curious, solving problems, assuming responsibility, being creative, and constructing meaning . . . This involvement produces a perception that the learning task is authentic"(AEE, no date).

From the time of John Dewey and William Kilpatrick to today, this purposeful and learner-centered process has been misinterpreted to mean a lack of guidance and instruction from the teacher. Sweller, Kirschner, and Clark (2007) in their article "Why minimally guided teaching techniques do not work: A reply to commentaries," [10] for example, describe the approach as "minimal guidance" where "process- or task-relevant information . . . is available if learners choose to use it" (p. 76). This simply does not adequately describe the best practices in experiential education as Hmelo-Silver et al. (2007) were quick to note. Just because educators aim to design problems and projects that require open-ended inquiry, uncertainty, and high degrees of student ownership does not mean that content-rich background knowledge, direct instruction, and teacher guidance are not part of the process. These are central aspects to experiential facilitation and we will discuss the practicalities of this in subsequent chapters.

It is clear that PBL is on the rise on college and university campuses. The Google Ngram reader of the term "problem-based learning" aptly demonstrates this (see Figure 3.6).[11]

As with integrated learning and our other core methodologies in the ecosystem of experiential education, there are some readily apparent reasons for this. Academic curriculum continues to move toward interdisciplinarity and the blurring of the lines between disciplines. Neuroscience, sustainability, and public health, for example, present pressing societal and research-related concerns that require multiple-disciplinary perspectives to address. In addition, the traditional disciplines themselves are increasingly collaborative (biologists need to understand and use computation science, for example). This curricular

60

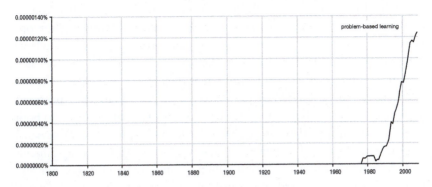

FIGURE 3.6 Google Ngram of "problem-based learning"

blurring is well suited to project-based approaches. In addition, PBL can help students develop tangible work-related knowledge, skills, and abilities. Many work environments mirror the PBL approach (how many work environments look like a lecture hall?). "Life *is* projects," says Art Heinricher, Dean of Undergraduate Studies at Worcester Polytechnic Institute—an institution noted for the use of PBL across the curriculum (personal communication, 2014; see case study below). As colleges and universities aim to better prepare graduates for the world of work, PBL represents a pedagogical approach that matches up well with that goal.

Finally, PBL seems to resonate strongly with the present-day "millennial" generation in terms of how they want to learn and to what ends. Given the weight of societal issues and concerns in front of them, this generation appears to have less tolerance for "learning for learning sake" and seem to push harder for relevance and application. As Bowen (2012) states: "[c]onstantly demonstrating relevance, making connections to interesting ideas and information, and inspiring study remain some of the most important strategies a professor can adopt" (p. 130). For these and other reasons, PBL has gained significant traction as a pedagogical approach on college and university campuses. And, as one of our core methodologies within experiential education, it strongly demonstrates the potential value and impact of experiential approaches in the college context.

Faculty Case Example of Project-based Learning: Karlyn Crowley, St. Norbert College

Karlyn Crowley, Professor of English at St. Norbert and Director of the Cassandra Voss Center for Women's and Gender Studies at St. Norbert College, uses what she describes as a "really simple but powerful" project in her Women and Gender Studies course to connect students to the real-world implications of the themes they are exploring in class. In her course, Crowley has students complete a project she refers to as the "gender log" where, for ten days they document three experiences of gender that they notice each day—whether that happens to be on TV, in the cafeteria, in discussions with peers, or anywhere else on- or off-campus during that time. The students have to both keep this log and, importantly, theorize the log by moving between the personal and theoretical using class content. As Crowley noted: "this is really difficult to do for students but it is a critical skill in identity studies because your text is the world around you" (2015, personal communication). Crowley continued: "this has consistently been one of the most powerful assignments I have ever done." When asked why she teaches experientially, she noted: "students retain the material better, they are more focused and engaged. But, really, I do it because it's more fun—both for me and my students. And, fundamentally, good teaching is about joy." Crowley's gender log is a reminder that project-based learning need not be huge in scale—simple but effective PBL assignments can be infused directly into a semester course with powerful results.

Institutional Case Example of Problem-based and Project-based Learning: Worcester Polytechnic Institute

Worcester Polytechnic Institute offers a compelling example of PBL across the curriculum and scaffolded developmentally from first year to fourth year. The original model, established in the late 1960s, involves two major projects—the IQP and the MQP. The IQP (Interactive Qualifying Project) occurs in a student's second or third year and "challenges students to address a problem that lies at the intersection of science or technology with society. During the IQP, students work in interdisciplinary teams, often with an external sponsoring organization, to develop solutions to real world problems" (Heinricher, 2015, personal communication). The MQP (Major Qualifying Project) is a nine-credit senior capstone experience.

> For engineers, it is usually a capstone design project. For other students, it is often a more traditional research project. It often becomes "experiential" because . . . there is an external sponsor or customer. A math major could analyze loss data for an insurance company or develop a routing algorithm for a high-volume call center [for example]
>
> (Heinricher, personal communication)

WPI recently added another project-based learning experience in the first year—the "Great Problems Seminar" which focuses on some designated global problem and combines interdisciplinary thematic study. The end result of WPI's curricular structure is a focus on PBL that builds from the first year to the fourth year with multiple and iterative project-based learning experiences.

CONCLUSION

What I have hoped to do in this chapter is paint a landscape of learning related to experiential education in the college context. As we have seen, there is quite a bit of variability and even confusion about terminology and typology in the literature and, while it is worth trying to sort out, it is not worth attempting to defend rigid and artificial definitional boundaries divorced from practice. As the Whitman quotation at the beginning of this chapter reveals, experiential education is indeed "large" and "containing multitudes." I have attempted to sort this out by identifying four core methodologies used in experiential education: active learning, community-based learning, integrative learning, and project-based learning. While there are a whole host of other terms used in relation to experiential education—terms such as collaborative learning, service learning, place-based learning, etc., I believe the four methodologies above encapsulate the larger conceptual categories of the ecosystem such that other terms can be placed as subsets within them. This conceptual "tidying up" is all well and good but there is a larger point to be made as we conclude our exploration of this landscape of learning. In the end, it is not about the methodologies themselves. It is about the purposes those methodologies serve. It is about answering some of the fundamental questions of educational philosophy: what are the purposes of education? And what knowledge is of the most worth?

Taken in isolation, experiential education as expressed through these methodologies doesn't really challenge the dominant structures of higher education. And the present context of higher education certainly makes for a compelling case for significant change. As Benson, Harkavy, and Puckett argue in *Dewey's Dream* (2007):

> For universities and colleges to fulfill their great potential and really contribute to a democratic . . . revolution, they will have to do things very differently than they do now. . . To become part of the solution, higher eds must give full-hearted, full-minded devotion to the painfully difficult task of transforming themselves into socially responsible *civic universities and colleges*. To do so they will have to radically change their institutional cultures

and structures, democratically realign and integrate themselves, and develop a comprehensive, realistic strategy.

(p. 84)

Experiential education, properly framed as a process of teaching and learning and not as an isolated method, pushes against some long standing, and increasingly ineffective, institutional structures in the academy. While there is certainly nothing wrong with specialization and tightly defined disciplinary expertise, taken too far, it has created a number of negative spill-over effects. From the "Ivory Tower" isolation between the campus and the community, increasingly narrow subject pursuits separated from societal concerns, and rigid departmental and administrative structures that dissuade collaboration and efforts at curricular coordination and integration, something more than just "methodology" needs to change in higher education. We will explore how to go about this deeper level of educational reform in Chapter 8. For now, we will conclude our explorations of the definitions and concepts of experiential education and shift our focus to more specific questions of the pedagogical approach.

NOTES

1. https://books.google.com/ngrams. Retrieved May 28, 2014. See Lin et al. (2012).
2. In my view, a "philosophy" of education has to sit on its own in terms of its epistemological, ethical, and ontological assumptions. In an earlier work (Roberts, 2012), I argue that experiential education draws from a variety of other philosophies and, as such, ought to be seen as derivative of them and not a philosophy in and of itself.
3. For other attempts at experiential nomenclature, see Gardner & Bartkus (2014), "What's in a name? A reference guide to work-education experiences"; and Mooney & Edwards (2001), "Experiential Learning in Sociology: Service Learning and Other Community-Based Initiatives."
4. https://books.google.com/ngrams/. Retrieved May 28, 2014. See Lin et al. (2012).
5. https://books.google.com/ngrams. Retrieved May 28, 2014. See Lin et al. (2012).
6. The 2014 AACU Annual conference in Washington, DC had a special focus on "New Designs for Integrative Learning" and Huber, Hutchins, & Gale (2005) initiated this discussion in their influential article, "Integrative Learning for Liberal Education."
7. https://books.google.com/ngrams. Retrieved June 16, 2014. See Lin et al. (2012).
8. www.insidehighered.com/news/2013/05/15/career-services-it-now-exists-must-die-new-report-argues, Retrieved March 16, 2015.
9. The College of Wooster "APEX" program, Augustana College's CORE program, the Center for Experiential Learning at Loyola University, and Earlham College's

Center for Integrated Learning are just a few examples of these new administrative structures. See the Appendix for more information on such centers and initiatives.

10. Yet again, in this title, we see the conceptual confusion around terms in experiential education.

11. https://books.google.com/ngrams. Retrieved May 16, 2014. See Lin et al. (2012).

REFERENCES

Ambrose, S. (2014). Personal communication.

Ambrose, S. A., Bridges, M. W., DiPietro, M., Lovett, M. C., & Norman, M. K. (2010). *How Learning Works: Seven Research-Based Principles for Smart Teaching* (1st ed.). San Francisco, CA: Jossey-Bass.

Association for Experiential Education (AEE). (No date). Retrieved April 23, 2014, from: www.aee.org/about/what-is-ee

Benson, L., Puckett, J. L., & Harkavy, I. (2007). *Dewey's Dream: Universities and Democracies in an Age of Education Reform, Civil Society, Public Schools, and Democratic Citizenship.* Philadelphia, PA: Temple University Press.

Bonwell, C. C., & Eison, J. A. (1991). *Active Learning: Creating Excitement in the Classroom* (1st ed.). San Francisco, CA: Jossey-Bass.

Bowen, J. A. (2012). *Teaching Naked: How Moving Technology out of your College Classroom will Improve Student Learning.* New York: John Wiley & Sons.

Boyer, E. L. (1997). *Scholarship Reconsidered: Priorities of the Professoriate* (1st ed.). San Francisco, CA: Jossey-Bass.

Bransford, J., Brown, A., & Cocking, R. (Eds.) (2000). *How People Learn: Brain, Mind, Experience, and School.* Washington, DC: National Academies Press.

Brevard. (No date). Brevard College Mission Statement. Retrieved April 30, 2014, from: www.brevard.edu/

Bringle, M. L., Kafsky, J., & Keiser, M. (2015). Personal communication.

Caine, R. N., & Caine, G. (1991). *Making Connections: Teaching and the Human Brain.* Alexandria, VA: Association for Supervision and Curriculum Development.

Chan, A. (2013). A roadmap for transforming the college-to-career experience. Retrieved March 15, 2015, from: http://rethinkingsuccess.wfu.edu/files/2013/05/A-Roadmap-for-Transforming-The-College-to-Career-Experience.pdf

Crowley, K. (2015). Personal communication.

Daloz, L., Keen, C. H., Keen, J. P., & Parks, S. D. (1996). *Common Fire.* Boston, MA: Beacon Press.

Duch, B. J., Groh, S. E., & Allen, D. E. (2001). *The Power of Problem-Based Learning.* Sterling, VA: Stylus.

Freire, P. (1970). *Pedagogy of the Oppressed.* New York: Continuum.

Gardner, P., and Bartkus, K. (2014). What's in a name? A reference guide to work–education experiences. *Asia-Pacific Journal of Cooperative Education, 15*(1), 37–54.

Heinricher, A. (2015). Personal communication.

Hmelo-Silver, C. E., Duncan, R. G., & Chinn, C. A. (2007). Scaffolding and achievement in problem-based and inquiry learning: A response to Sweller, Kirschner and Clark (2007). *Educational Psychologist, 42*(2), 99–107.

Huber, M. T., & Hutchings, P. (2004). *Integrative Learning: Mapping the Terrain.* Washington, DC: Association of American Colleges and Universities.

Itin, C. M. (1999). Reasserting the philosophy of experiential education as a vehicle for change in the 21st century. *Journal of Experiential Education, 22*(2), 91–98.

Larmer, J. (2014). Project-based learning versus problem-based learning versus x-bl. Retrieved January 24 from: www.edutopia.org/blog/pbl-vs-pbl-vs-xbl-john-larmer

Lin, Y., Michel, J.-B., Aiden, E. L., Orwant, J., Brockman, W., & Petrov, S. (2012). Syntactic annotations for the google books ngram corpus. Proceedings from the ACL 2012 systems demonstration.

Mazur, E. (1997). *Peer Instruction: A User's Manual.* Upper Saddle River, NJ: Prentice Hall.

Mazur, E. (2015). Personal communication.

Meadows, D. H. (2008). *Thinking in Systems: A Primer.* White River Junction, VT: Chelsea Green Publishing.

Monterola, C., Roxas, R. M., & Carreon Monterola, S. (2009). Characterizing the effect of seating arrangement on classroom learning using neural networks. *Complexity, 14*(4), 26–33.

Mooney, L. A., & Edwards, B. (2001). Experiential learning in sociology: Service learning and other community-based learning initiatives. *Teaching Sociology, 29*(2), 181–194.

Orr, D. W. (2002). *The Nature of Design: Ecology, Culture, and Human Intention.* Oxford: Oxford University Press.

Pelligrino, J., & Hilton, M. L. (2012). *Education for Life and Work: Developing Transferable Knowledge and Skills in the 21st Century.* Washington, DC: National Research Council.

Rorty, R. (1998). *Achieving Our Country: Leftist Thought in Twentieth-Century America.* Cambridge, MA: Harvard University Press.

Saltmarsh, J., Hartley, M., & Clayton, P. H. (2009). *Democratic Engagement White Paper.* Boston, MA: New England Resource Center for Higher Education Publications.

Stein, M. (2014). Personal communication.

Sweller, J., Kirschner, P. A., & Clark, R. E. (2007). Why minimally guided teaching techniques do not work: A reply to commentaries. *Educational Psychologist, 42*(2), 115–121.

Vandergrift, E. (2015). Personal communication.

Chapter 4

The Instructional Paradigm

Leaving Safe Harbors

> A ship is safe in the harbor, but that is not what ships are for.
> (William G. T. Shedd, quoted in Shapiro, 2006)

INTRODUCTION

I recently took up playing the banjo. I had always loved the sound of the banjo and I had had previous experience playing both the guitar and the ukulele so I was excited to give my new Gold Tone a try. I learned quickly that a banjo is neither a guitar nor a ukulele. It has similarities to each one, but the differences are substantial enough that I felt like a fish out of water for the first couple of weeks. The stringing of a banjo sits almost in between a five-string guitar and the four-string ukulele. The picking technique and the chord structures are completely different. It is oddly similar and different at the same time.

Learning how to teach experientially offers an analogous situation in my view. It is still teaching—something that if you are reading this book I assume that you have some experience with. It looks familiar—there are lesson plans and units, teachers and students, classroom contexts, assessments and grades—yet experiential education can also feel very different, and even awkward at times. For those of us who have been socialized into college level teaching, who are used to playing that specific instrument in some fairly routinized ways, picking up this similar-yet-different form of teaching requires some new thinking, new techniques, and importantly, some shedding of old habits and patterns. Any time that happens in life, it feels initially very uncomfortable and even scary. I am reminded of a faculty member who once confided to me in a faculty development workshop:

I *like* my house, I like the rooms in my house. It feels comfortable to me and I've spent a lot of time getting it the way I like it. Now you are asking me to move out. I understand that there may be good reasons to move out, but it's not easy.

Indeed, many of us understand how much energy it takes to move—both into and out of actual houses and homes and into and out of various habituated teaching approaches. We teach to a large extent based on how we were taught. This process begins in grade school and carries forward, with increasing influence, through graduate school. As Jose Bowen (2012) writes:

We were all taught with lectures, and we all give them despite a mountain of evidence showing that they are poor transmitters of content and even worse tools for learning. When our students learn, we attribute their learning to our current methods. We persist because common sense tells us that lecturing is working. But any analysis of how we might improve student learning has to start with a dissection of everything we currently do.

(p. xi)

We have learned the strings, the picking style, and the chord progression. We are comfortable with it and we think it makes pretty good music. Picking up a new instrument, especially for those of us who may be pre-tenure, or even for those of us who have been teaching for more than a decade, can be a very scary thing. No one wants to hear a poor rendition of *Twinkle, Twinkle, Little Star*, after all.

However, learning requires change. Albert Einstein once said, "[t]he significant problems we face cannot be solved at the same level of thinking that we were at when we created them" (quoted in Barr and Tagg, 1995, p. 1). It is a great irony that we teachers readily admit we are sometimes the worst students. Ask anyone who does faculty development work and they will say that teacher-participants can be far worse than students in terms of their resistance to new content, their classroom comportment, and their openness to different ways of doing things. We are in the learning business yet we ourselves are sometimes the most fearful of failure and the most resistant to change. The quotation by William G.T. Shedd that begins this chapter serves as a reminder as to the imperatives of risk-taking—"a ship is safe in the harbor, but that is not what ships are for." Teaching without openness to significant change and learning is also safe, but it is not what teaching is meant to be. As Parker Palmer (1998) notes while citing Albert Camus:

Camus speaks of the fear we feel when we encounter something foreign and are challenged to enlarge our thinking, our identity, our lives– the fear that lets us know we are on the brink of real learning: "It is the fact that, at a certain moment, when we are so far from our own country. . . we are seized by a vague fear, and an instinctive desire to go back to the protection of old habits . . ."

(p. 39)

Real learning comes from risk and some measure of fear. We know this intuitively in regards to our students—can we mirror it in our teaching selves?

In what follows, we will explore four key changes that a teacher needs to consider in moving into a more experiential approach to teaching and learning. Note that I said "more experiential." It is not the case that someone either is or is not an experiential educator, in my opinion. There is a continuum of competence that one moves through as you gain more experience and more familiarity with experiential approaches. That being said, in order to start being "more experiential" there *are* some dominant paradigms in education (and in particular higher education) that really must be left behind. The four paradigms we will explore are: The Instruction Paradigm; The Seat Time Paradigm; The Teacher as Expert Paradigm; and The Primacy of Content Paradigm. For each of the four paradigms discussed below, I have added an experiential principle to consider in contrast. These are meant to encourage new ways of thinking and approaching educational moments and spaces with our students. The chapter will conclude with a suggested new role for college and university faculty members of the future—as curators of experience. If we are to leave behind these paradigms, these "safe harbors," where are we leaving them to go toward? By my reckoning that new horizon line is to learn how to curate experience and the chapter will finish with an exploration of this concept.

THE INSTRUCTION PARADIGM

The first paradigm, or safe harbor, to leave behind is the notion that, as Robert Barr and John Tagg (1995) wrote: "A college is an institution that exists to provide instruction" (p. 1). This "Instruction Paradigm" permeates nearly every corner of the academy and is a subtle yet profoundly powerful driver of the way we approach teaching and learning. According to Barr and Tagg, the Instruction Paradigm can be identified by:

- teacher-centered content delivery;
- transfer of knowledge one-way from faculty to students;

- a focus on courses and programs;
- success and effectiveness defined through course evaluations (teaching);
- a focus on end-of-course assessments (summative assessments);
- faculty and students working independently and in isolation.

Despite sustained critique from many quarters—both inside and outside the academy, the instruction paradigm remains a dominant paradigm in higher education today.[1] So much so that we sometimes hardly notice it is there. It is like asking a fish to notice the water it exists in, but attempt to disrupt it, and the structures and mindsets become much more visible. As Barr and Tagg argue:

> The teaching and learning structure of the Instruction Paradigm is atomistic. In its universe, the "atom" is the 50-minute lecture, and the "molecule" is the one-teacher, one-classroom, three-credit-hour course. From these basic units the physical architecture, the administrative structure, and the daily schedules of faculty and students are built . . . The resulting structure is powerful and rigid . . . It is antithetical to creating almost any other kind of learning experience. A sense of this can be obtained by observing the effort, struggle, and rule-bending required to schedule even a slightly different kind of learning activity, such as a team-taught course.
>
> (p. 8)

Leaving this paradigm behind requires significant work at the personal and institutional level, and there is strong evidence that this shift is happening. We will discuss the implications for institutional-level changes in Chapter 8. For now, we will focus on what we can most easily control—our own mental models of teaching and learning.

Barr and Tagg contrast the Instruction Paradigm with what they term the "Learning Paradigm." They argue:

> To say that the purpose of colleges is to provide instruction is like saying that General Motors' business is to operate assembly lines or that the purpose of medical care is to fill hospital beds. We now see that our mission is not instruction but rather that of producing learning with every student by whatever means work best.
>
> (p. 1)

In Barr and Tagg's analysis, the Learning Paradigm contrasts with the Instruction Paradigm in the following ways.

TABLE 4.1 Comparison of Learning Paradigm and Instruction Paradigm (Barr and Tagg)

Instruction Paradigm	Learning Paradigm
Teacher-centered content delivery	Student-centered learning
Transfer of knowledge one-way from faculty to students	Student discovery and construction of knowledge
A focus on courses and programs	A focus on creating powerful learning environments
Success and effectiveness defined through course evaluations	Success defined through demonstrated student learning outcomes
A focus on end-of-course assessments and "private" assessment	A focus on iterative and developmental feedback and "public" assessment
Faculty and students working independently and in isolation	Collaborative, cooperative, supportive, and cogenerated work

Learning to teach more experientially absolutely requires moving from the Instruction Paradigm to the Learning Paradigm—from the left column to the right column. Doing so requires spending more time attuned to our students and perhaps less time focused on our content. And this brings us to a key experiential principle: teach people, not content.

EXPERIENTIAL PRINCIPLE #1: TEACH PEOPLE, NOT CONTENT

The experiential education principle that responds to the Instruction Paradigm most directly is to "teach people, not content." Of course, there is not a simplistic dichotomy between the two but this principle encourages us, as teachers, to place the primary point of emphasis on learners and learning, and away from a myopic focus on content. Just because you "taught" content, it doesn't mean your students learned it. This is why experiential educators place a good deal of emphasis on the environment that surrounds the content, not just the content itself. Teaching people and not content reorients us to pay more attention to the living beings in our presence, to design educational experiences that are centered on them, and gives them opportunities to discover and construct new knowledge with each other and with you. Teaching people and not content means focusing less on what you know as an instructor, and focusing more on the learning you can facilitate with your students. This includes viewing the classroom as a learning community, ensuring that learners see the relevance in the material, have a safe and supportive social atmosphere,

71

and have multiple opportunities to publicly practice out and demonstrate new learning. Finally, this principle asks us, as faculty, to consider education as a holistic process—one that involves seeing students as not just "brains on a stick" but as physical, emotional, and spiritual beings who want to be seen as such. As Deborah Meier once argued, teaching is listening and learning is talking. Leaving the safe harbor of the instructional paradigm and entering the riskier waters of the learning paradigm asks that we spend more time listening and less time talking—more time understanding our students and how they learn and less time delivering content. How we do this while still maintaining and developing a strong, intellectually vibrant educational atmosphere is where the science meets the art of teaching and learning.

THE SEAT TIME PARADIGM

Following from this fundamental shift from instruction to student learning, there are three more paradigms and safe harbors to leave behind. The "seat time" paradigm is pervasive in the K–12 world but also holds sway in higher education as well. Learning, by this logic of thinking, happens only (or perhaps predominantly) in fixed places and times when students are in seats in a classroom. Any time taken away from "kids in seats" is time spent away from real learning. Connected to this paradigm, and one I hear a lot in faculty development workshops, is the "depth versus breadth" debate. "This all sounds good," a given faculty member may say, "but my discipline is too content rich to allow for spending all this time doing things experientially. I need to get through a lot of content and I have a short time to do it in." There are at least two arguments against the seat time paradigm—one pedagogical and the other market-based. The problem with the "seat-time, heavy content" paradigm is that it is just not supported by the research. This is especially true as we learn more from the field of neuroscience about learning and the brain. As Bowen (2012) notes:

> the traditional passive method of college teaching (i.e. lecturing) is less effective than active learning in developing higher order cognitive skills. Delivering content alone has virtually no effect on students' beliefs about the world. Students can memorize data that conflict with their beliefs, but without active engagement with the new material, in the form of discussions, writing, debates, projects, and hands-on application, they do not really confront the implications of the new content.
>
> (p. 92)

Pedagogically, heavy content delivery in a passive format is ineffective not only in terms of knowledge retention but in helping students transfer learning, acquire higher-order thinking skills, and develop metacognitive skills such as learning to understand (Bransford et al., 2000). No less than the American Academy for the Advancement of Science supports this view. In recommendations given to biology faculty in higher education, they argue that "we need to put the depth versus breadth debate behind us." Because biology is so often considered a "content heavy" discipline that must spend a lot of time in direct instruction, this particular quotation is worth citing in some length. It demonstrates that these paradigm shifts are occurring in every discipline.

As biology faculty, we need to put the "depth versus breadth" debate behind us. It is true today, and will be even more so in the future, that faculty cannot pack everything known in the life sciences into one or two survey courses. The advances and breakthroughs in the understanding of living systems cannot be covered in a classroom or a textbook. They cannot even be covered in the curriculum of life sciences majors. A more tenable approach is to recast the focus of biology courses and curricula on the conceptual framework on which the science itself is built and from which discoveries emerge. Such a focus is increasingly interdisciplinary, demands quantitative competency, and requires the instructor to use facts judiciously as a means of illustrating concepts rather than as items to be memorized in isolation.

The time has come for all biology faculty, but particularly those of us who teach undergraduates, to change the way we think about teaching and begin to develop a coordinated and sustainable plan for implementing sound principles of teaching and learning.

(p. xv, 2009)

Moving away from the seat time paradigm does not mean we dismiss things like direct instruction or the importance of sequential memorization of facts in certain disciplines. It simply suggests that allowing such methods to dominate our approaches in the classroom flies in the face of 21st-century evidence-based teaching and learning. By focusing more on concepts (rather than on discrete facts), social and collaborative learning (rather than individual work), and on metacognition (rather than just memorization), we can better facilitate both knowledge retention and transfer.

The second argument against the seat time paradigm is more market-based. In the age of the Internet, MOOCs, and distance education, a seat time, content delivery paradigm of learning leaves one extremely vulnerable to "outsourcing." Here is what one university dean said during a radio interview: "With modern technology, if all there is is lectures, we don't need faculty to do it. Get 'em to do it once, put it on the web, and fire the faculty" (Hanford, no date). There are far more efficient and cost-effective ways to deliver content in today's world. If students can access a lecture on the history of the labor movement in the United States from an internationally renowned scholar on the subject in an online format, why would they or should they bother coming to class and listening to you at 8:30 in the morning on a Thursday? The rise of online content providers such as Study.com, Udacity, Coursera, and Kahn Academy demonstrate that direct instruction is easily and effectively replicable and scale-able through the worldwide web. Faculty and institutions would be wise to seriously consider what else they are offering besides expert driven content delivery to justify the value of their position (and possibly the position of the institution as a whole). To do so, however, means we have to be unusually disciplined about not just *how* we teach but in *what* we teach—which brings us to our next experiential principle.

EXPERIENTIAL PRINCIPLE #2: LESS IS MORE

To do experiential education well, a teacher has to accept the principle of "less is more." As we will learn in the coming chapters, experiential approaches *do* require more time: more time for students to explore, inquire, and work their way through content; more time for teachers and students to reflect on what they are experiencing and learning; and more time for students to develop and present authentic learning products and projects. Time is perhaps the single biggest coin of the realm for a teacher. We often exclaim that "we have no more time" to do this and then point over at the administrators and demand some concession that is very difficult to produce—"unless we change the academic calendar and the faculty load system, we can't do this kind of teaching." Without dismissing these issues (which are real and significant), I think we often forget that, by and large, we faculty are the ones in control of our classroom content and curriculum. We are the ones choosing to declare that we must (must!) cover all this content in our classrooms, courses, and majors. But the reality is that, except in rare circumstances, we really don't have to cover everything we think we do. And we do, in fact, have more latitude and freedom to "do more with less" in our classrooms should we choose to take it. To do so, we have to let go of content "coverage" and think more carefully about student outcomes. Robert Fried (2001) suggests one exercise to encourage this kind of thinking. In *The Passionate Teacher*, he tells a story of working with a group of teachers where he asks them how it would change their approach to classroom content if their teaching effectiveness were assessed by how much their students recalled one year after taking their class. As Fried recalls, the teachers were incredulous—as they chuckled, they responded that such an assessment approach would change virtually everything they would do in the classroom. So, what is it that you want your students to know a year after they take your class? Design your class and your content to those outcomes and strip off the rest. This is the mindset behind McTighe and Wiggins (1998) "Enduring Understandings" in the Understanding By Design (UbD) model. They ask teachers to consider in their planning of courses and content: "What are the big ideas? What specific understandings about them are desired? What misunderstandings are predictable?" (p. 22).

THE TEACHER AS EXPERT PARADIGM

Connected to each of the two previous paradigms is the "teacher as expert" paradigm. In this paradigm, the teacher is seen as the central location of expertise and it is through the process of teaching that at least some of that expertise transfers from professor to student. Paulo Freire famously referred to this as the "banking method" of schooling. In the teacher as expert paradigm, knowledge is viewed as something that is stored within the teacher and subsequently "deposited" into the student through schooling. Freire (1970) noted that

> [n]arration (with the teacher as narrator) leads the students to memorize mechanically the narrated content. Worse yet, it turns them into "containers," into "receptacles" to be "filled" by the teacher. The more completely she fills the receptacles, the better a teacher she is . . . Education thus becomes an act of depositing, in which the students are the depositiories and the teacher is the depositor.
>
> (p. 72)

This idea is easy to visualize and, perhaps, even easier to vilify. Many a student in an introductory course on educational theory has come into contact with Freire's ideas for the first time and finally come to understand something that has bothered them their entire life about how schooling is organized. But despite its seductive pull, the Banking concept of education has also been used, simplistically in my view, to argue that direct instruction should play no part in the educative process—in essence, throwing the baby out with the bathwater. It is not direct instruction, as a method, that is at issue here any more than Freire's ideas should be seen as simple classroom methods. As Donaldo Macedo notes in the introduction to the 2000 edition of *Pedagogy of the Oppressed*: "Even many liberals who have embraced [Freire's] ideas and educational practices often reduce his theoretical work and leading philosophical ideas to a mechanical methodology" (p. 10). It is not methods that we should be focused on but rather the orientation to knowledge in educational spaces—who has it, and how it is constructed. The "teacher as expert" paradigm views knowledge as one-way transmission rather than a multifaceted construction between the teacher, the learners, and the subject matter. As Parker Palmer (1998), argues in *The Courage To Teach*:

> our conventional pedagogy emerges from a place that is hardly communal. It centers on a teacher who does little more than deliver conclusions to students. It assumes that the teacher has all the knowledge and the students have little to none, that the teacher must give and the students must measure up. Teachers and students gather in the same room at the same time not to experience community but simply to keep the teacher from having to say things more than once.
>
> (p. 116)

Leaving behind this paradigm is essential to move into more experiential pedagogy principally because experiential work with students frequently requires the teacher to learn alongside her students. This, then, leads us to an important experiential principle.

EXPERIENTIAL PRINCIPLE #3: LEARNING ALONGSIDE

Experiential education asks the teacher to move away from a paradigm that views knowledge as expert-driven content held exclusively by the teacher and "banked" into students. But this is easier said than done. Content expertise is supposed to be the *raison d'être* of a Ph.D. We are hired, as professors, because of our command of a particular body of knowledge. Popular culture holds out an image of the university professor as someone comfortably in command of their field—capable of inspiring and impressing young minds with the depth of their expertise. But scratch the surface of that popular image and take a walk on many college and university campuses and you will see a very different reality. In fact, *many* of us teach things we are most decidedly *not* experts in. And importantly, we can still teach effectively. Therese Huston, in her book *Teaching What You Don't Know* (2009), notes:

> [c]ollege and university faculty members often find themselves having to teach what they don't know. They have to get up in front of their classes and explain something that they learned just last week, or two days ago . . . But stories like these can't be found in books on teaching, most of which

begin with [the premise] (1) to teach well, you need to have mastered the subject matter . . . Can you be a good teacher before you've mastered the subject matter? Or, perhaps while you're mastering it? I believe the answer is yes. Plenty of faculty members teach outside of their expertise and do it well.

(p. 2)

If we can leave the "safe harbor" that says we are experts and that we should only teach that which we have mastered and that we must transmit this, one-way, to our students, we can enter into the risky but rewarding terrain of learning alongside students and, in so doing, create a very different yet very effective educational environment. This does not mean that we have to reject the idea of subject expertise or content mastery. But experiential education asks us to be *more comfortable* than perhaps we have been previously with the idea of learning alongside our students, allowing content to be "uncovered" rather than "covered," and for students to spend more time actively constructing knowledge and less time passively receiving it from the instructor. For Palmer, this means going beyond the simplistic dichotomies and tired arguments of either the "teacher-centered" classroom or the "student-centered" classroom and finding a third way. He calls it the "subject-centered classroom" where the subject itself serves as the important "third thing" that collapses the false dichotomy of the teacher-student relationship.

The subject-centered classroom is characterized by the fact that the third thing has a presence so real, so vivid, so vocal, that it can hold teacher and students alike accountable for what they say and do. In such a classroom, there are no inert facts. The great thing is so alive that the teacher can turn to student or student to teacher, and either can make a claim on the other in the name of that great thing. Here, teacher and students have a power beyond themselves to contend with—the power of a subject that transcends our self-absorption and refuses to be reduced to our claims about it.

(p. 117)

Leaving the safe harbor of the teacher as expert paradigm and learning alongside our students is foundational to becoming more of an experiential educator. Palmer's subject-centered framework also reminds us that such a move does not simply shift control entirely on to students but rather adds a third element—that of the subject matter itself—as the center of knowledge creation.

THE PRIMACY OF CONTENT PARADIGM

The final "safe harbor" to leave behind involves the Primacy of Content paradigm. When I work with teachers on experiential education, I often hear a response like this one: "I already do experiential learning in my classroom. I have taken my students on field trips, we have completed experiments in the lab, and I have brought in guest speakers to talk about the real-world connections to what we are learning—all that is experiential." This is all true. This particular faculty member is doing some version of experiential learning in a variety of ways. However, a key attribute is missing here. Typically in this mental model, "hands-on" experiences in classrooms and courses are often secondary to content delivery—they are used to provide a "break" from regular classroom instruction or to "spice things up." The experiential component, in this paradigm, is often not the central focus of the learning process or, worse, it devolves into "activity for activity sake." As Dewey (1938) notes: "An experience may be immediately enjoyable and yet promote the formation of a slack and careless attitude" (p. 26). Field trips, in class active games, and other forms of "hands-on" learning may indeed be novel and can be used as "edutainment" but it does not necessarily follow that these activities are as educational as they could be.

I refer to this as the "Primacy of Content" paradigm. A Religion professor might lecture on ethics and have students role play in class. A Political Science professor might go through a unit on alternative energy policy and then go out to visit several renewable energy project sites locally or regionally. Or an institution might have a "service learning" experience as a graduation requirement but without any kind of meaningful integration into a student's intellectual life. These all serve as perfectly fine experiences in and of themselves, but they all tend to view experience as somehow isolated and separated from intellectual inquiry. Barr and Tagg's "instructional paradigm" remains mostly unchallenged. The philosophical approach of experiential education asks us to leave this relatively safe harbor and try a different approach. Rather than design experiential learning as an "activity" or as something "extra" or (worse) completely disconnected from content, experiential education asks the teacher to design for educational experience as the *central point of focus*. What does it look like to place student experience at the center of the curricular endeavor? It means designing first and foremost for powerful educational experiences for your students rather than looking for "extra" experiences that supplement content. It means designing your course to mirror the "real-world" as much as possible. And it means purposefully constructing "messiness" into the educational process.

In a draft statement on "Principles and Practices of Integrated Liberal Learning" produced by the American Association of Colleges and Universities in 2013, the authors state: "integrative liberal learning *prepares students to tackle complex and unscripted problems*—to apply evidence-based reasoning, judgment and ethical responsibility to questions where the answer is not known and the consequences matter" (p. 2, emphasis added). The key here is the idea of preparing students to tackle "complex and unscripted problems." The best way to prepare students for such problems is to design authentic learning environments that replicate, as closely as possible, that particular context.

In the world of leadership theory, this is often referred to as "naturalistic decision making" (Galloway, 2007). Research supports the approach that if you want someone to learn how to make good decisions, you must have them practice making decisions in contexts that are as authentic as possible to the real thing. This is why flight simulators are crucial to pilot training. They replicate the conditions pilots experience in the air. They also typically simulate "complex, unscripted problems" to test pilots ability to think on their feet and make sound judgments. This is a classic experiential learning environment. Pilots experience something—say, a malfunction of some sort they were not anticipating—and then they go about responding to it. Later, with an instructor, they debrief what happened and the instructor may highlight key principles or content pieces that the pilot may wish to study more carefully for the next simulation. One could imagine flipping this scenario—the pilot learning about the anticipated malfunction from the instructor *first* and then experiencing it in the simulator. There is nothing inherently wrong with this approach. But it is not naturalistic and it will likely be less effective at helping that pilot learn to deal with complex, unscripted problems outside the simulator because the problem was well scripted and known ahead of time. The pilot knew exactly what to expect. In the Primacy of Content paradigm, our students enter our classrooms and learning environments *knowing exactly what to expect*. So, how do we flip that script?

EXPERIENTIAL PRINCIPLE #4: EXPERIENCE BEFORE LABEL

The experiential principle of Experience Before Label suggests one way to respond to the Primacy of Content paradigm. In this principle, we place primacy on designing complex, messy, unscripted "experiences" before we tag those experiences with content (labels). This allows students to enter the learning process from a stance of active inquiry and investigation—what just happened? Why did it happen? What do I need to know to figure this out?

The Association for Experiential Education explains this principle by stating that: "Experiences are structured to require the learner to take initiative, make decisions and be accountable for results." And "[t]hroughout the experiential learning process, the learner is actively engaged in posing questions, investigating, experimenting, being curious, solving problems, assuming responsibility, being creative, and constructing meaning" (Association for Experiential Education, no date).

Research supports the effectiveness of this approach. As we discussed in Chapter 1, Kuh's (2008) work on High Impact Learning Practices demonstrates that many of the learning environments that we would consider to be "complex and unscripted" are the same environments where students report the most learning and the biggest impact: research experiences, community-based learning, study abroad, and internships. Each of these practices place experience at the center of the educational endeavor. Student research opportunities are all about "experiences before labels"—such an approach is at the heart of learning the scientific method.[2] Students immerse themselves in messy, unscripted, and complex problems and then, with the help of a knowledgeable guide (the advising faculty member), work their way through the mystery. Community-based learning experiences ask students to reflect on and meaningfully connect what they are doing in the community with academic content. Study abroad is one big "experience" as well as a collection of smaller "experiences" that often challenge students with a whole host of unscripted, complex, and messy issues to try to work through. Internships give students opportunities to see the real-world implications of what they are studying and learning in the classroom. Again, designed well, all such experiences set the student up for integration and reflection into new learning, content, and concepts. According to Brownell & Swaner (2010), students participating in these types of experiential high-impact practices have a set of positive outcomes including "higher grades, higher persistence rates, intellectual gains, greater civic engagement, increased tolerance for and engagement with diversity, and increased interaction with faculty and peers" (AACU LEAP Vision for Learning, p. 16). Significantly, Kuh's research also found that historically underserved students appear to get more benefits from such experiential engagements than majority students. In other words, while these practices are beneficial to all students, they appear to be extraordinarily beneficial to underserved students.

Designing for the primacy of direct experience can be one of the hardest adaptations for a teacher, in my experience. We are used to a classroom routine where we are in more control—we select the content, the assignments, and the assessments well ahead of time and the students enter into the education space to then "experience" those labels. While I have known a few radical colleagues who wait to design their syllabus until they know who their students are, most of us are more than a little uncomfortable with the notion of "co-created" syllabi. But should we be? Bowen notes:

> faculty want students (1) to master the content of the course and (2) to learn how to use that content in some way . . . Most of us wish we had more time to spend on the latter; however, class time gets taken up with the former, and higher-end processing of the content gets sacrificed.
>
> (p. 103)

The well-cited "flipped classroom" approach is one way to respond to the Primacy of Content paradigm by taking content delivery (label) out of class time and replacing it with more processing and testing out (experience) in class. The point with the Experience Before Label principle in experiential education is, as Bowen notes, to find more ways for students to use, test out, question, and explore the content *and* to do so in a way that draws out their inherent curiosity. Research in neuroscience, for example, clearly indicates the importance of emotion, practice, and relevance to engagement and long-term memory storage in learning (Brembs et al., 2002; Draganski et al., 2004; Pert, 1997; Zull, 2004). By focusing on the principle of experience before label, we can design learning environments that give students more such opportunities.

CONCLUSION: TEACHERS AS CURATORS OF EXPERIENCE

If we decide to leave behind these paradigms and set sail out from our safe harbors, where exactly are we sailing to, and what new skills and abilities must we learn and practice along the way? The future horizon line for higher education, in my view, is to view teachers not as content providers but as "curators of experience." Knowing your subject matter is a necessary but not sufficient quality of being an exceptional teacher. The ability to lecture charismatically is a handy tool for any teacher but, again, it is not enough given our unique educational moment. More than anything else, the 21st-century teacher has to be an expert curator. As Bowen notes:

> [t]he job of faculty needs to become more focused on designing learning experiences and interacting with students. While we, as faculty, consider ourselves as course designers, we still mostly deliver content . . . Faculty must become curators, performers, directors, assemblers, and pedagogues.
>
> (p. 247)

81

To "curate," in this sense, speaks to the knowledge, skills, and abilities associated with the design and meaningful organization of experience. When we think of a museum curator we often think of someone responsible for preserving, maintaining, and interpreting a "collection." But we also might think of how particular "shows" or "exhibits" are curated. An effectively curated show is one in which the museum visitors experience is amplified and made more powerful through the meaningful organization and facilitation of the experience. One can think of the new 9–11 museum in New York or the Holocaust museum in Washington, DC as exceptionally curated "experiences" for those who go through them. It is not enough to simply aggregate collections without thought or purpose and hope that attenders get something from the experience. Effective, even transformational, shows and exhibits come from expert curation—from someone (or a group of people) thinking carefully and intelligently about what goes in, what is left out, and how to meaningfully arrange the content in such a way as to amplify the experience for the attender.

As we have discussed, if facts and information of all sorts are readily available to students, teachers are not needed to deliver said facts. We have smart phones, tablets, and networked computers that can deliver data and information at a far greater speed and at far greater scales of cost-effectiveness than a teacher in a classroom. So what are teachers for, then? Data and information are not synonyms for learning and education. A teacher is the person who, working collaboratively with students, moves the conversation from data and information to knowledge and wisdom. The world is awash in data and information, and in desperate need of more knowledge and wisdom. The transformative teacher of the 21st century will learn to curate experiences with and for students while taking advantage of all the resources—online and otherwise, at their disposal. Community-based learning, active learning, integrated learning, project-based learning—many of the methods we consider experiential cannot be readily outsourced to the Internet *generically*. They require a knowledgeable teacher who can help meaningfully curate both content *and* high impact experience, and know when to apply which context and for what purposes. Viewing teachers as curators of experience does not mean we reject online, blended educational opportunities. Bowen states:

> If teaching is largely about faculty–student interaction, then we have to recognize that human interaction is changing. Our interactions with students (and with each other) are now all hybrid. We will need an equally hybrid strategy for creating courses that leverage the best of each world.
>
> (p. 49)

We need to place online learning in proper perspective and understand when it is of best use and when it is a tool poorly applied. Working in physically situated teams, dialoguing across differences, listening respectfully, and interacting in public, social, spaces are all vital for democratic life. In the end, our students must not learn that "hell is other people."

So, what kind of skills and abilities are required for a teacher to be an effective curator of experience? This will be the subject of the next three chapters of this book. Thus far, we have worked through the landscape of experiential education in the college and university context, examining some of the seismic shifts that have recently occurred that shape the current conversation on teaching and learning. We have made an attempt to "pin down" experiential education both in terms of operational definitions and in terms of the specific methodologies that fall under its organizational and conceptual structure. Finally, in this chapter, we have discussed several key mental models or paradigms that must be left behind in order to move into more experiential forms of teaching and learning. This sets the stage for a series of chapters that give concrete, practical suggestions and advice for designing, facilitating, and assessing experiential education in the college context. They include "design skills" such as framing, lesson and unit plan development, and back-mapping. They include "facilitation skills" such as processing reflection and guided inquiry, group development, and conflict resolution. Finally, they include "evaluation skills" such as formative and summative assessment strategies, demonstrations of learning, and designing authentic learning products. These concrete, practical skills are the fundamental building blocks necessary to "curate experience" in the college classrooms of the future.

NOTES

1. It is worth noting that Barr and Tagg's article "From teaching to learning—A new paradigm for undergraduate education" came out in 1995—almost 20 years from the time of this writing.
2. It is also no surprise that Dewey himself was quite enamored with the scientific method as an operative metaphor for the educational approach for which he was arguing.

REFERENCES

Association for Experiential Education (AEE). (No date). Retrieved April 23, 2014, from: www.aee.org/about/what-is-ee

Barr, R. B., & Tagg, J. (1995). From teaching to learning? A new paradigm for undergraduate education. *Change: The Magazine of Higher Learning, 27*(6), 12–26.

Bowen, J. A. (2012). *Teaching Naked: How Moving Technology out of your College Classroom will Improve Student Learning.* San Francisco, CA: Jossey-Bass.

Bransford, J., Brown, A., & Cocking, R. (2000). *How People Learn: Brain, Mind, Experience, and School.* Washington, DC: National Academies Press.

Brembs, B., Fred D., Reyes, F. D., Baxter, D. A., & Byrne, J. H. (2002). Operant reward learning in Aplysia: Neuronal correlates and mechanisms. *Science, 296*(5573), 1706–1709.

Brownell, J. E., & Swaner, L. E. (2010). *Five High-impact Practices: Research on Learning Outcomes, Completion and Quality.* Washington, DC: Association of American Colleges and Universities.

Dewey, J. (1938). *Experience and Education.* New York: Collier Macmillan.

Draganski, B., Gaser, C., Busch, V., Schuierer, G., Bogdahn, U., & May, A. (2004). Neuroplasticity: Changes in grey matter induced by training. *Nature, 427*(6972), 311–312.

Freire, P. (1970). *Pedagogy of the Oppressed.* New York: Continuum.

Fried, R. L. (2001). *Passionate Teacher.* Boston, MA: Beacon Press.

Galloway, S. (2007). Experience and medical decision-making in outdoor leaders. *Journal of Experiential Education, 30*(2), 99–116.

Hanford, E. (No date). Rethinking the way college students are taught. Retrieved June 16, 2014 from: http://americanradioworks.publicradio.org/features/tomorrows-college/lectures/rethinking-teaching.html

Huston, T. (2009). *Teaching What You Don't Know.* Boston, MA: Harvard University Press.

Kuh, G. D. (2008). *Excerpt from High-Impact Educational Practices: What They Are, Who Has Access to Them, and Why They Matter.* Washington, DC: Association of American Colleges and Universities.

Macedo, D. (2000). Introduction to the anniversary edition. In P. Freire (Ed.), *Pedagogy of the Oppressed* (pp. 11–28). New York: Continuum.

Palmer, P. J. (1998). *The Courage to Teach: Exploring the Inner Landscape of a Teacher's Life.* San Fransciso, CA: Jossey-Bass.

Pert, C. B. (1997). *Molecules of Emotion: Why you Feel the Way you Feel.* New York: Simon & Schuster.

Shapiro, F. R. (2006). *The Yale Book of Quotations.* New Haven, NJ: Yale University Press.

Wiggins, G. P., & McTighe, J. (2005). *Understanding by Design.* Alexandria, VA: Association for Supervision and Curriculum Development.

Zull, J. E. (2004). The art of changing the brain. *Educational Leadership, 62*(1), 68–72.

Principles and Practices of Experiential Education

PART 2

Principles and Practices of Experiential Education

Chapter 5

Design and Experiential Education

> The complexity of design work is often underestimated. Many people believe they know a good deal about design. What they do not realize is how much more they need to know to design well, with distinction, refinement, and grace.
>
> (John McClean, quoted in Wiggins and McTighe, 2005)

INTRODUCTION

Good design is fundamental to all teaching and learning. If you are a teacher, you probably have experience with the basics of educational design—from small-scale projects like lesson or unit planning, to larger scales such as an academic major or even general education across the institution as a whole. Design, in many ways, is what teachers do. But, as John McClean notes in the quotation that begins this chapter, doing design and doing design *well* are two different things. This is particularly the case when considering design in experiential education. Consider the following real-life vignettes:

1. University students on a mandatory service project travel to a blighted neighborhood in a large, metropolitan city in the United States. There, they help work on a Habitat for Humanity house for the day. Upon concluding their work that afternoon, the faculty chaperone overhears two women students as one says to the other, "Hey! Take a picture of me in front of this house over here—this is *so ghetto!*"
2. A group on a semester academic study abroad program in New Zealand spends three weeks on a tour of the South Island visiting

many interesting locations and sites along the way. In the post-program report at the end of the semester, the professor notes that the trip felt like an "extended bus tour" and that it seemed to have no "academic connection whatsoever to the program."

3. A small-scale experiential farm program that had been in existence for over thirty years runs afoul of college administrators after several incidents involving risk management and safety. A lengthy review of the program ensues and a 40-page report is generated including budget, administrative structure, and academic connections. Missing from the report, however, was any reference to specific learning outcomes aligned with the proposed activities.

Each of these vignettes reveals the challenges of designing experiential education well. In the first example, it is clear that the context of the learning has not been properly framed for the students (combined perhaps with the fact that the service experience was mandatory in the first place). In the second example, it seems as though the extended "study tour" of the South Island of New Zealand was heavy on "tour" and light on "study," and that the trip was not well designed to purposefully integrate that experience into the rest of the academic semester. In the last example, the farm-based experiences articulated in the proposal were clearly rich and rewarding for the students but, in the end, fell short of demonstrating outcomes aligned with the college mission. Each example, in other words, has within it some "design failure" as it relates to doing experiential education well. This chapter, then, is about understanding the principles and practices of experiential education design such that you can design well—perhaps even with the "distinction, refinement, and grace" that McClean mentions (though in my experience such lofty heights are rarely reached in teaching). In what follows, we will first discuss how to "get ready" to incorporate an experiential education initiative, component, or course, including key elements of effective educational design that cross over from more traditional to experiential contexts. Then, we will discuss several principles and practices of design that are specific to experiential education. We will conclude this chapter with an experiential design frame that can be adapted to a variety of contexts and scales.

BACKWARD DESIGN

Wiggins and McTighe's landmark text, *Understanding by Design* (2005), launched renewed attention to the idea of design in education. In their analysis, the problem with most educational design is an over-emphasis on "twin sins":

designing for activity-focused teaching and designing for coverage-focused teaching. They go on to note: "Neither . . . provides an adequate answer to the key questions at the heart of effective *learning*: What is important here? What is the point? How will this experience enable me as a learner to meet my obligations?" (p. 3). We have already discussed the issues with one of these sins throughout this book—that of coverage-focused teaching, but it is worth noting that, within the context of experiential education, the far more likely "sin" of educational design is activity-focused teaching. Ritchhart, Church, and Morrison (2011), in their book *Making Thinking Visible*, argue that:

> In the often misunderstood notion of experiential or inquiry-based learn-
> ing, students are sometimes provided with lots of activities. Again, if designed
> well, some of these activities can lead to understanding, but too often the
> thinking that is required to turn activity into learning is left to chance. Often,
> the activity itself is little more than a palatable form of practice.
>
> (p. 9)

In the vignette above about the semester study-abroad program in New Zealand, for example, the three-week "study tour" of the South Island was clearly much too activity focused. The faculty member leading the semester could clearly see that in retrospect. The challenge, though, is to think through a design orientation that avoids these "twin sins" of activity-heavy and content-heavy education. A central way to do this—both within experiential design and educational design more broadly, is, as Stephen Covey (1989) noted, "to begin with the end in mind."

Beginning with the end in mind in almost all educational contexts means a focus on the kinds of learning goals or outcomes you mean to achieve first. Only after these have been clarified does the educator "back-map" to the kinds of activities, content, and processes that have the best chance of achieving those results. This kind of thinking is, of course, not new in education (see Tyler, 1959) but it never ceases to surprise me how often we fail to actually implement this design principle in practice despite mounting evidence of its importance. One significant reason for this is that, as Fink (2003) notes about college instructors, "most of us have had little or no training in how to design courses" (p. 1). Whatever the reasons, beginning with the end in mind has not been the accepted tradition in course and lesson plan design. As Wiggins and McTighe note: "We are advocating for the reverse of common practice . . . We ask designers to start with a much more careful statement of the desired results—the priority *learnings*—and to derive curriculum from the performances called for or implied in the goals" (p. 17, emphasis in text).

89

Let's return to the "design failure" vignette above about the experiential farm program to illustrate this point. The working group of faculty, students, and administrators spent the better part of a year thinking through all the various elements and components of a relaunching of a successful farm program down to aligned academic coursework, acreage, supervision, and budget. The final report was detailed and comprehensive. Yet absent in the document was any notion of backward design. What, in the end, do we want students, faculty, and staff to *learn* through these activities and experiential initiatives? The working group, in retrospect, became caught up in designing an engaging, experiential program full of activity and missed a critical point of educational design—beginning first with desired outcomes and then matching those up with appropriate educational processes.

Anyone involved in assessment issues in higher education today will note the heightened emphasis on learning outcomes. Curriculum mapping, rubrics, and logic models are becoming familiar terms in departments, divisions, and programs. Much of this is driven by reforms generated through accreditation processes and assessment initiatives. The Association of American Colleges and Universities LEAP (Liberal Education and America's Promise) initiative, for example, argued that we must be far more intentional about outcomes when we design educational experiences:

> The council further calls on educators to help students become "intentional learners" who focus, across ascending levels of study and diverse academic programs, on achieving the essential learning outcomes. But to help students do this, educational communities will also have to become far more intentional themselves—both about the kinds of learning students need, and about effective educational practices that help students learn to integrate and apply their learning.
>
> (p. 5, 2007)

It is important, at this point, to note that we must not get too technocratic with backward design. Only teaching those things that are readily assessable is a poor substitute to artful educational design. Most of us who teach in higher education care about things that have a much longer maturation cycle than a semester. A colleague of mine in the Philosophy Department once asked a workshop leader in a session on educational assessment: "Tell me, how do you assess a turned soul?" What he was getting at is the fact that sometimes the most important learning does not translate well into a ready-made rubric. That being said, it is important not to throw the proverbial baby out with the bathwater. Backward design is useful precisely because it forces us to think about how students are to demonstrate the learning we most care about. Ignoring this brings us back to Wiggins and McTighe's "twin sins"—an over-emphasis on content coverage on one hand or activity on the other. This is especially true for experiential design. Because experiential education is often dismissed or marginalized in the context of higher education, it is all the more important to demonstrate how the activities and processes you have designed speak to common learning outcomes and objectives. Missing the mark on this important principle leaves one vulnerable to legitimate critiques of designing "fun" but marginally effective educational experience. Having communicated (I hope) the importance of backward design in any educational context, there remain several other key principles that are particularly useful in experiential design and we turn to those now.

PRINCIPLES OF EXPERIENTIAL DESIGN

Beyond the emphasis on learning outcomes and back-mapping, effective experiential design requires a careful consideration of several specific principles that, in my experience, can often make the difference between success and failure, and between educational adequacy and educational "art." These design principles include:

1. Making the invisible, visible: the art of framing.
2. Theirs to ours to theirs: the art of empathy.
3. Chunking: the art of beginnings and endings.
4. The gum and the chewing: the art of ownership.

These principles of experiential design are borrowed and adapted from a wide range of source material. Like most folks who ply the teaching craft, I am always on the lookout for concepts, ideas, and models that I can adapt to my own educational context. Some of these come from the K–12 landscape, some come from the experiential education world, while others are so hybridized at this point I cannot even recall where they came from, but each of them in my experience represents an essential orientation to effective experiential education design. When I have participated in post-mortem evaluations and reviews of programs or experiences "gone bad," I can almost always identify that one (or more likely several) of these principles were ignored or inappropriately applied. One of my earliest mentors, a teacher-educator by the name of Mark Reardon, used to say: "Your design is your outcome." In many ways, this is sage advice. While paying attention to these design principles may not ensure success, it certainly creates the opportunity for educational experience to happen. Consequently, it is worth exploring each of these in some depth.

91

Making the Invisible, Visible: The Art of Framing

In the first vignette about the service-learning trip to the blighted neighborhood, it was clear that whatever the organizers thought would be the outcomes of the experience, they got something entirely different. In this case, an attempt to expose privileged college students to some of the issues of economic disparity and social justice wound up reinforcing negative stereotypes (when two of the students made light of how "ghetto" the neighborhood looked at the conclusion of the experience). While there are likely lots of elements to critique in terms of experiential design, a critical one is the idea of "framing." Framing, in experiential education, refers to how you overtly set up the experience with your students as a learning endeavor. Too often, we simply assume that students know why it is they are going through a given experience. Without proper framing, students muddle through educational experiences without much sense of why they are doing certain things or how they connect. Consider, for a moment, how we do (or, in this case, do not) frame the "liberal arts" for students in the United States. We assume our students know what the "liberal arts" are and why they might be important to their education. As a result, we don't spend all that much time framing this for incoming first years. It is no surprise, then, that getting an undergraduate at most U.S. colleges and universities to articulate a definition and value statement around the "liberal arts" is an act of futility. General education courses become courses to "get out of the way" rather than essential experiences to become a fully educated global citizen. Frames matter. They strongly influence how learners approach experiences and what kinds of outcomes they tend to take away. "Making the invisible, visible," as a design principle, simply means paying careful attention to how you are framing the activity or process by making your learning outcomes and your educational purposes intentional and overt to your students, both at the beginning and throughout.

Two examples from my own teaching may help reveal this principle. In 2008, my wife and I led an environmental studies semester program to New Zealand. Both of us had experience leading "field" courses previously and one of the things we like to emphasize is the importance of collaborative group work. As a result, we purposefully design into the experience opportunities for students to live and work together outside the classroom context—there are times on the program where they live in close quarters with each other, participate in various group chores such as cooking and cleaning, and generally live in an immersive social group setting. We knew why we wanted to design the program that way—the social dynamics of learning included holistically in this way has always yielded huge benefits on the programs we led. Students learn how to work together, to dialogue across differences big and small, and understand experientially that problem solving is always a messy social endeavor. Learning this matters for students interested in environmental problems and problem solving. Yet in this particular case, we failed to frame this well to our students (for many of whom this was their first experience with "experiential education"). Because of this design failure on our part (not making the invisible, visible), we had a near group mutiny at the beginning of the program as students voiced frustration with having to do chores such as cooking and cleaning—they simply saw no purpose in doing so and thought that it was unnecessary to their overall experience. Once we listened to their concerns and reframed the reasons behind the design, things went much better.

Another example comes from an entirely different context. For many years I taught a course titled "Foundations of Education"—a class that explores the philosophical, historical, and sociological issues around public schooling in the United States. Typically, I would have a wide range of students in the class —from sophomores to seniors. They also had a wide range of academic backgrounds and experiences in schooling. It should come as no surprise that I always designed the course with a fair amount of experiential work—from an embedded service learning experience, to group projects, to in-class simulations. Invariably when it came time for me to read the course evaluations, I would get the same bimodal feedback—a sizable chunk of the class absolutely loved the experiential components and considered it a highlight of the course and semester but they hated the times when I would lecture. An equally sizable chunk hated the experiential components and wished I would just lecture more. It took me a while, but I finally came around to realizing that I was not making the reasons for my course design overt to my students— I was not making the invisible, visible. After this realization, I both placed in the syllabus and emphasized throughout the semester the importance of diverse learning styles and pedagogy, and discussed openly why I design the course the way I do and what I anticipate will be the outcomes for the students. After this simple change, the bimodal evaluations I was used to seeing were reduced significantly (though you always wind up with some true believer students and some you will never please).

The point is that good framing sets students up for transformative experiences. It puts questions into their heads that they can then bring to the learning. A good frame invites the student in. But be careful, you can also "over-frame." Spending too much time framing an experience is disengaging. A good frame puts students in an anticipatory state. Over-framing is, in essence, a bad form of lecturing. Recall the worse "tour guide" you have ever experienced. It was probably someone who over-framed the experience by talking too much, giving too much detail, or generally beating the joy out of the possibilities for open exploration. Frames can be shorter or longer depending on the size of the curriculum project. A 55-minute class might have a five-minute frame. A semester-long study abroad might spend several weeks "framing" the experience (including the orientation period).

One final point and suggestion: remember that designing effective experiential education does not require trips to "exotic" locales—it can happen anywhere so long as it is properly framed. One approach I have found useful in this regard is to think about how to "make the familiar, strange." Richard Kraft (1995), in his essay "Closed classrooms, high mountains, and strange lands," argues that "strange lands" experiences are important for students because they "change not only the environmental setting but take away most of the linguistic, cultural, religious, political, and other cues with which we have grown accustomed"(p. 158). Designing for a "strange lands" experience does not have to necessitate some international study trip or even leaving the classroom itself. If we think of "strange lands" as a state of mind rather than a physical location it opens up the possibility for any number of experiential applications. Any time, as educators, we can design a process with and for our students that makes the "familiar, strange," we have increased the likelihood for engagement and higher impact learning. A well-designed simulation puts the learner into a "strange lands" state where the normal context of the classroom is transformed into a new imaginative space. Anyone who has experienced a classroom environment where the students seem to get "lost" in the simulation or even at times, completely overtaken by the role they are playing understands how, through good design, a classroom can become a "strange land."

Beyond the classroom, a more conscious effort to make the curriculum in higher education more "place-based" by working with the local community where the college or university is situated also highlights the pedagogical power of the strange lands design principle. In my own courses, I am consistently amazed at how little my students know about or participate in the life of the community outside campus. A van ride to a local farm, a community survey project where they must interact with locals, or a service learning experience often sparks a "strange lands" reaction from students—confusion, wonderment, and a heightened sense of engagement and appreciation for the context of their learning. Importantly, this takes careful framing.

Designing for a strange lands experience means paying attention to the ways in which you can heighten the sense of novelty and imagination in students through experiential components. There is a reason that students find off-campus study experiences so engaging and transformative. The goal of "making the invisible, visible" is to seek ways and opportunities to bring strange lands experiences and other resourceful cognitive states into educational spaces regardless of location and scale. Framing, done well, amplifies educative experience in a 55-minute class as much as it does on a three-week January travel term. Finally, framing is especially important in getting students to think critically about educative experiences they are having. Too many study abroad programs seem to fall into the trap of glorified travel tours rather than carefully framed exercises in academic, critical thinking. Designed and framed well, such experiences can truly be transformative for students. As Lamson and Merline (2015) note:

> Reflection in this context is treated as a substantive critical reasoning skill. Inevitably, students reflect on questions of race, class, language, power, privilege, age, gender, and self as they relate to the experiences they have lived throughout the semester. The question of what it means to be human after the dehumanizing experiences they have seen are often at the heart of their discussion. They struggle to negotiate privilege, how to make sense of it, and how to incorporate thoughtfully that privilege into their own lives.

Importantly, such reflections only happen if the experiences have been framed well from the beginning—through attention and care to educative design.

When I approach experiential course design, I often think through the following questions to help me ensure that I am "making the invisible, visible" and paying careful attention to effective framing:

1. What are my key learning outcomes? What would I like students to remember three–five years after this course or experience?
2. What prior knowledge do my students have on this subject?
3. What pre-exposure to the content or subject will peak their curiosity?
4. How can I make the relevance of this clear and overt but simultaneously intriguing and exploratory?
5. Where are there opportunities for students to be placed in "strange lands" states of mind?

Theirs to Ours to Theirs: The Art of Empathy

Another crucial principle in experiential design is the "Theirs to ours to theirs" model. Too often, in our common education practice, students are required to enter our world as professors and faculty members with little to no acknowledgment of their world as students. Several years ago I was reminded of this when I needed to go in to one of the student dormitories on campus to find a student. Entering into that building was an intimidating experience. Everything was unfamiliar to me—the layout of the commons, the hallways, the incredibly tiny rooms, not to mention the smells. I felt timid and on guard—something I typically don't feel in my usual work world of academic buildings. Reflecting on this experience, I realized that what I felt in that moment was likely what students felt when they entered *my* world. It helped explain why students who I would see being loud and boisterous after class were sometimes quiet and meek in class. At its most broad, this is really about empathy—taking the time to consider where your students are coming from, what they know, what they care about, who they are, and to walk awhile in their shoes as you go about your experiential design. This is not necessarily easy and can be a place of discomfort for us, as teachers. As bell hooks (1994) noted:

> During my twenty years of teaching, I have witnessed a grave sense of dis-ease among professors (irrespective of their politics) when students want us to see them as whole human beings with complex lives and experiences rather than simply as seekers after compartmentalized bits of knowledge.
>
> (p. 15)

However, extending our empathy in this way helps us to be better curriculum designers—of that, I am sure.

The best framework I have found to do this is the "Theirs to ours to theirs" model. Effective experiential education requires that you consciously design educational experience to move from their world (the world of the learner) into "our" world (the world of the learner and teacher together), and back into "their" world (transferring the learning to novel contexts). Let's discuss each of these stages in turn. Beginning in "their" world in experiential design means paying particular attention to relevance and creating a sense of "invitation" into the learning. What previous experiences or knowledge do students have on the subject? What questions might they bring with them? What is relevant in their world? What misconceptions could they have? Beginning in "their" world means giving students a sense of relevance with the educational process as well as honoring their previous learning and experience (some of which, importantly, may be incorrect). The "ours" stage of the principle refers to the ways in which new content and learning is experienced. Notice here that the operative term is "ours" and not "mine."

Thinking of students experiencing "my" class or "my" content sets up a divide that we would like to avoid when practicing experiential education. Seeing the new learning and experience as "ours" allows for the environment to be more collaborative and less hierarchical. One teacher describes her approach this way: "I propose situations for people to think about and I watch what they do. They tell me what *they* make of it rather than my telling them *what to make of it*" (Brooks and Brooks, 1999, p. 5). Finally, in the second "theirs" stage, we are actively encouraging students to make the new learning their own by assimilating it with other knowledge and experience, by thinking through possibilities for application and transfer, and by marking it with personal meaning and significance. As designers, we might think through questions such as: Where does this new learning integrate with other knowledge and experience for students? In what ways can they apply this new learning? How can this new learning, through reflection and synthesis, be made significant for students? Making this process of integration and transfer overt in the educational design ensures that students will be both aware of it and asked to demonstrate it.

Consider the following example of putting the "Theirs to ours to theirs" principle into practice in experiential design. A senior capstone experience in biology includes a senior seminar class. The faculty member in charge of the class decides to design student-led, small group research projects into the seminar. The faculty advisor first convenes the entire class and frames the overall experience of the semester and the anticipated learning outcomes. She then asks the students to form "affinity" groups around research topics of interest. For the next several weeks, students meet, confer, and debate on what research topics they will explore together and how they will use their research to demonstrate the learning outcomes of the senior seminar. With the instructors' assistance, students form into several independent research groups around topics of interest for the students. For example, one group will be using a case study of a national park in Ecuador to reveal intersecting issues and concepts of conservation biology, while another group will be exploring the biochemistry of lead poisoning. Throughout the semester, the groups meet independently with the instructor and progress is monitored. Students also are asked to team teach a class for the rest of the students that explores their particular research topic through reading key journal articles and papers on the subject. At the conclusion of the semester, student groups present their findings to the campus community at the weekly biology colloquium lunch hour where their peers and faculty advisors listen and ask follow-up questions about their research. Some questions in the presentations were technical (about the specific nature of their research) but some were more personal ("What did you gain from this experience?"; "How does this research connect to other courses and experiences you've had?").

In this fairly basic example of experiential design, the instructor first began in "their" world by facilitating a process where student interests combine with desired learning outcomes from the faculty member. Then she moved the process into the "our" world stage by designing multiple opportunities for co-learning and teaching as new context is explored and learned. Finally, she moved the experience back into "their" world by creating an opportunity for students to demonstrate their new learning in a public presentation where they had to both own the new learning *and* think about how it might transfer to new contexts. Below are some queries to consider when designing experientially.

1. How well do I know my students—their background, interests, and previous experience? How can I capture that information as early as possible in order to help design educative experiences (theirs)?
2. What can we do together, as part of this course, activity, or experience? Where might there be opportunities for me, as the teacher, to learn alongside my students (ours)?
3. Where will students go after this course or experience? How can I design opportunities for them to explicitly make connections to other experiences, content, or future aspirations (theirs)?

Chunking: The Art of Beginnings and Endings

Chunking refers to how you can organize the content and activities of the learning experience in meaningful ways. Consider the following list of letters:

IBFVTNOJBLKFJ

Try to memorize them as presented. Now look at the next list of letters:

JFK, LBJ, ON, TV, FBI

The second list is much easier to memorize, isn't it? Yet this is the same list of letters reorganized back to front that have been "chunked" and arranged in a meaningful way that draws on previous experience and information. Our students often experience our content and activities, metaphorically, like the first list of letters—a long list of "things" that they find difficult to assimilate and retain. Creating more "beginnings and endings" through chunking gives learners a structure that lets them see how things are meaningfully organized and that draws from previous experience. Chunking taps into the brain's natural tendency to seek out patterns and meaning making in new experiences. In your experiential curricula designs, look for natural beginnings and endings that you can capitalize on and make overt to students.

For example, I often use a "big picture" map to encourage this overt "chunking." Remember that your students do not have the same view of a course, lesson, program, or experience that you do. Provide them with a big picture as soon as possible at the beginning of the experience. Rather than an exhaustive outline or itinerary, the big picture gives your students a taste of what is coming and allows them to begin making patterns, connections, and frames for the experience. It is helpful to have it on a visual and I often use a "you are here" map with a movable arrow. Revisit the big picture throughout the experience to further solidify the pattern. This is, in essence, an adaptation of the old "tell them what you are going to tell them, tell them, and tell them what you told them" adage but with a more modern, less didactic spin.

Chunking can happen at any scale—you can "chunk" lectures, courses, semesters, or entire four-year developmental plans for students. Assignments themselves can be chunked by staging them out and provided feedback and assessment during each stage. Rather than wait until the end of an experience to reflect on it, you might design in smaller reflective "chunks" along the way. For example, internship experiences often benefit from some chunking whereby students are asked to reflect prior to beginning the internship, early on in the experience, and then at prescribed intervals throughout. Staging out the reflections in this manner can anticipate potential trouble spots, particularly at the beginning of an experience when norms are being established.

Here are some other questions to consider as you think about how you might chunk small activities and large, multiday experiences in your experiential designs:

1. Are there natural "beginnings and endings" that I can see in my course or experience that I can chunk?
2. How can I conceptually organize or label these chunks in ways that help students make patterns and meaning?
3. What are the ways I can make these beginnings and endings in my course design overt to my students?

The Gum and the Chewing: The Art of Ownership

I recently spoke with a colleague in economics who was excited about incorporating a new community-based research component into his Urban

Political Economy course. He was interested in dividing his class into five groups, each of which would research historical and contemporary data on a neighborhood here in Richmond, Indiana, to build a baseline set of data for a more longitudinal research agenda. As we discussed his idea, it became clear that this project was much bigger than a simple "20 percent of the total grade" kind of assignment. To do this project well, he needed to dedicate more time to manage the groups, more time for the groups to interact in the community, and more time for iterative feedback on their research process. Investing this time meant reducing content from what he traditionally covered in his course. He believed the end result would be worth it, but he was still struggling with how to fit it all in. What my colleague was wrestling with, from my perspective, was the experiential design principle of "the gum and the chewing."

If we think of the content we typically cover in a given course or class as "the gum," then the chances for our students to actively work with and reflect on that content is "the chewing." What experiential education asks of us is to design for less gum and more chewing. This can be very difficult for us as teachers as we learned in the previous chapter. But cramming an experiential component into an existing course without providing sufficient time for process and reflection is a common design failure in experiential education. It is like putting too much gum in your mouth. The joy of gum is not the gum itself but the act of chewing. In experiential design, we must design for multiple and sufficient opportunities for students to experience chewing—doing so means we must be extra diligent about how much gum (content) we are presenting as part of the class or course. This is as much about the concept of "ownership" than anything else. In experiential education, we want students to "own" the learning. Ownership, in this sense, means to make the content "my own" by having opportunities to work with it (chew it). The more we try to cram in, the less time students have to make it their own.

Returning to the conversation I had with my economics colleague, we talked about staging the assignment throughout the semester so that students had opportunities for formative assessment of learning (rather than making it a stand-alone assignment among many others in the semester). We talked about the need for my colleague to leave open times in the syllabus for the groups to meet, work, and discuss where they were on their research. For my colleague, he had to do some more thinking about what content in his course was truly the most important and what content he could jettison. And he had to think about how to weave the content into the research experience such that students were overtly asked to make connections between the economic theories and modes of analysis of the course and the community-based research projects.

This is not easy work and it often requires us to let go of long-held beliefs and assumptions about the primacy of content over process in educational design. However, one thing I have found to be true in working on this design issue over the years—I have yet to hear a faculty member who, after purposefully creating more "chewing time" and less "gum," came back to say that their students were "bored" or that they "ran out of things to do" in the course. Take a risk—design more chewing and less gum into your course and see what happens. Some suggestions I have found useful in applying the "gum and chewing" principle of experiential design:

1. Use backward design to determine what enduring understandings, significant learning, and outcomes are the most important in the course or unit.
2. Go "big" by choosing one experiential project or activity that forms the backbone of the entire semester (rather than discrete and disconnected experiential activities crammed into your existing course content).
3. Go "small" by trying one, smaller experiential project, unit, or activity in your semester as a kind of pilot test. I have often found that faculty find this safer and, after realizing the benefits, expand the project in subsequent semesters.
4. Purposefully design in "flex days" that allow you to be flexible to the needs of the experiential process, whether that means more time for reflection or more time for group process and organization.
5. Ask yourself: how can I make the chewing more significant, more intentional, more powerful in this class, course, or unit?

"EELDRC": AN EXPERIENTIAL DESIGN FRAME

After considering effective educational design and several specific principles in experiential design, we turn now to an experiential design frame that puts it all together. The "EELDRC" (I pronounce it like "Eel Doctor See") design frame is an adaptation from a model first used by Deporter, Reardon, and Singer-Nourie in their book *Quantum Learning* (1999). I have introduced it to faculty in a variety of contexts—from K-12 teachers to college and university faculty—and, invariably, I hear back that they find the simple model to be both memorable and useful in thinking through experiential education design. The acronym stands for:

Enroll
Experience
Label
Demonstrate
Review/Reflect
Connect

The design frame can be used at any scale—from the micro scale of a lesson in a class to the macro scale of an entire semester or even the sequence within a major course of study. We will walk through each part of this design frame using an example of an experiential activity I used in my Environment and Society course to teach the idea of the "tragedy of the commons." The activity I used was a fishing simulation called "The Harvest"[1] where teams of students act as competing fishing boats in a given fishery. Each "round" of the simulation is a "year" and, through the process, they inevitably overfish the existing resources. In the discussion afterwards, we typically talk about what caused the collapse of the fishery. It is important to emphasize, again, that while this example is for a class period, the EELDRC frame lends itself to any scale— from the 55-minute class to the semester long project and beyond.

In the "Enroll" segment, we seek to engage students in the material through intrigue and answering the learner question "What's In It For Me?" Enrolling students in experiential education provides the frame, the sense of invitation, and the overt attention to learning outcomes. To enroll students in my tragedy of the commons class, I asked them to think of examples of things that are "owned by everyone and therefore owned by no one." Examples students gave included public schools and libraries, the Internet, parks, the air we breathe, etc. This was my attempt to start in their world. At some point I gave a more specific frame by stating: "Today, in class, we'll explore this idea of the commons and why it is important as we consider environmental problems and problem solving."

In the "Experience" phase, we aim to immerse students in a complex, open-ended, ill-defined, "messy" problem or project of some sort. It is crucial, at this point, that students explore and have the chance to experiment based on incomplete information or some other "messy" problem. In the example of the tragedy of the commons class, I introduced the Harvest simulation and set them up into teams. We went through the rules of the simulation and we launched right in to "fishing." I have done this simulation many times and the energy in the room is always high. Students are animated, discussing their catch rates, and trying to figure out the best strategies in their teams. During this phase, as the teacher, I am simply monitoring the simulation—making sure teams are on task and that the basic rules are followed. Usually, after 15–20 minutes, the various fishing-boat teams have fished the ocean completely out and they all groan as I announce that there are no more fish in the sea. It is important to note, here, that the simulation is not "fixed." Experiences that are overly scripted feel manipulative to students and you want to make sure that you keep to the spirit of open-ended problem solving. There *is* a way to fish the ocean sustainably, but the various fishing boats have to work together to determine catch limits. While one group may realize this, I have found that the competitive spirit often drives the other teams to ignore pleas of working together. This becomes an important discussion point in the reflection afterwards.

After the experience, use the "Label" phase to punctuate the most salient points with direct instruction and/or targeted discussion. In the example we have been exploring, I usually start the class discussion with a simple query: "What happened?" Students identify the key points quite readily: "We overfished"; "We didn't work together"; "We got greedy." But fairly quickly and with a little prompting from me, they move into connecting this to the broader issues and concepts of our class: "This kind of thing happens all the time—companies that have a profit motive are not incentivized to work with their competitors just like we were." After letting this discussion go on for awhile, I then shift into direct instruction with a prepared 15-minute "lecturette" on the tragedy of the commons concept and how it relates to environmental problems and problem-solving. The most important thing to emphasize here, in my view, is that the "label" phase comes *after* the "experience" phase. This is often a struggle for us as educators, as we discussed in Chapter 4. We have been socialized into a lesson plan sequence that first introduces content and then asks students to do things with it (labs, papers, etc.). However, in experiential design, you want to have students get into the content and concepts first through messy, complex, ill-defined problems and projects, and then bring them back into content. This is the "experience before label" principle of experiential education and is the single most important element of experiential design in my view.

Following the "Label" segment, we provide opportunities for the participants to "Demonstrate" the new learning to encourage connections and personalization of the material. Importantly, this involves the students demonstrating new learning to the teacher, not the other way around. In my lesson plan on the tragedy of the commons, I had them demonstrate prior course content on diagraming systems and systems thinking. In small groups,

I asked them to see if they could diagram the system of the Harvest simulation —what was the "stock"? What were the inflows and outflows? Where were the feedback loops and were they stabilizing or reinforcing? This exercise allowed me to see how they were understanding the basics of systems thinking and also to see if they could incorporate those understandings in a novel context (through the Harvest simulation).

In the next phase, "Review," we reinforce key learning, concepts, and connections explored over the course of the educational process. Returning again to my example class, I had student groups display their systems diagrams for the class and we walked through what elements of the diagrams accurately depicted the system and which ones didn't. I used this opportunity to clarify a few lingering questions—"What's the difference between stabilizing and reinforcing feedback again?"—and provided opportunities for students to comment on the class experience as a whole. The "Review" stage can be longer or shorter, based upon the quality of the experience and the length of time invested in the overall process. An intense semester-long study-abroad program will have a much different investment in the "Review" stage than a 55-minute class.

Finally, the "Connect" phase attempts to integrate the experience with other elements of the course or other elements of students' lives. In the case of my class, I set up the topic for the next class by leaving them with a series of Socratic queries: "Is the tragedy of the commons the only way to view environmental problems and problem-solving in society? Are commons always tragic? Can we think of commons issues that are not tragic? Why aren't they?" The "Connect" phase can be content based (as my example was) or it can be made more personal by asking students to consider the impact of the new learning on other parts of their life, other classes they are taking, or experiences they are having in college.

The EELDRC design frame is effective but it is not sacred. I violate the sequence all the time and sometimes I even leave out phases depending on the nature of the content or the educational process I was working with. But I have often found it very useful as I begin the experiential design process to carefully consider how I am responding to all the elements of the frame whether I do them exactly in sequence or not. Consider it a template and a place to start but certainly not the definitive approach to experiential design. The one place where I would encourage teachers to push themselves, though, as I mentioned above and in the previous chapter, is in working on putting the experience before the label. This, to me, is the heart of the experiential education process.

CONCLUSION

We began this chapter by emphasizing the critical importance of design in experiential education. To get beyond some of the common traps with the approach—becoming too focused on activities, improper framing of experiential processes, forgetting to plan in time for reflection and processing, and not giving sufficient ownership of the learning to students—we need to carefully consider the elements of good educational design. Because of experiential education's reputation for being "non-traditional" as a pedagogical approach, it is all the more important to clearly articulate the learning outcomes of various initiatives and to make those visible to students. Because of the temptation to focus on activities, we must make sure that activity is meaningfully integrated into course content. Finally, because we, as teachers, have been socialized into particular sequences and structures when it comes to lesson and unit planning, it is important to have a guide and template for experiential design that attempts to ensure that we are incorporating the key elements of the process into our planning. In so many ways, "your design is your outcome." However, as we will see in the next chapter, good design is a "necessary but not sufficient" element of effective experiential practice. A design, after all, is an inert structure. What makes it come alive are the skills and abilities of the teacher as he or she interacts with the design and with the students—this is what I call "facilitation," and we turn to the practicalities of that side of experiential education next.

NOTE

1. For more information on this simulation, see Sweeney & Meadows (2010). *The Systems Thinking Playbook.*

REFERENCES

AACU. (2007). *College Learning for the New Global Century.* Washington, DC: Association of American Colleges and Universities.

Brooks, J. G., & Brooks, M. G. (1999). *In Search of Understanding—The Case for Constructivist Classrooms* (revised ed.). Alexandria, VA: Association for Supervision and Curriculum Development.

Covey, S. R. (1989). *The 7 Habits of Highly Successful People.* New York: Fireside.

DePorter, B., Reardon, M., & Singer-Nourie, S. (1999). *Quantum Teaching: Orchestrating Student Success.* Needham Heights, MA: Allyn & Bacon.

Fink, L. D. (2003). A self-directed guide to designing courses for significant learning. Retrieved September 15, 2014 from: www.bu.edu/sph/files/2011/06/self directed1.pdf hooks, b. (1994). *Teaching to Transgress: Education as the Practice of Freedom*. New York: Routledge.

Kraft, R. J. (1992). Closed classrooms, high mountains and strange lands: An inquiry into culture and caring. In K. Warren, Sakofs, M., Hunt, J. (Eds.), *The Theory and Practice of Experiential Education* (pp. 8–15). Boulder, CO: Association for Experiential Education.

Lamson, P., & Merline, R. (2015). Global issues manifested in a local setting. In N. Sobania (Ed.), *Putting the Local in Global Education*. Sterling, VA: Stylus.

Ritchhart, R., Church, M., & Morrison, K. (2011). *Making Thinking Visible: How to Promote Engagement, Understanding, and Independence for All Learners*. New York: John Wiley & Sons.

Sweeney, L. B., & Meadows, D. L. (1995). *The Systems Thinking Playbook*. Burlington, VT: Chelsea Green.

Tyler, R. W. (1959). *Basic Principles of Curriculum and Instruction: Syllabus for Education 305*. Chicago, IL: University of Chicago Press.

Wiggins, G. P., & McTighe, J. (2005). *Understanding by Design*. Alexandria, VA: Association for Supervision and Curriculum Development.

Chapter 6

Facilitation and Experiential Education

When a word is deprived of its dimension of action, reflection automatically suffers as well; and the word is changed into idle chatter, into verbalism, into alienated and alienating 'blah' . . . On the other hand, if action is emphasized exclusively, to the detriment of reflection, the word is converted into activism. Men are not built in silence, but in word, in work, in action— reflection.

(Paulo Freire, *Pedagogy of the Oppressed*, 1970)

INTRODUCTION

In the summer of 1994, I sat in an unremarkable (and cold) hotel conference room near Oceanside, California, participating in a five-day teacher development workshop. We were learning, ostensibly, about the latest in "brain-based" teaching strategies. While I don't remember many of the content pieces from that workshop, one singular example stays with me to this day. The workshop leader had a picture of the space shuttle on a flip–chart and then proceeded to ask us about the basic elements of a rocket. We discussed many items but, in the end, it came down to some kind of a payload and a propulsion system. But the key distinction, and why I still remember it to this day, was the analogy the workshop leader made to teaching. You can have the right payload, he said, but without an effective propulsion system, the rocket won't go where you want it to go. Propulsion in educational contexts is all about the idea of facilitation. Without effective facilitation, the best laid educational plans lie lifeless on the ground. In the context of experiential education, the "payload" could be course content or it could just as easily be selected experiences or activities. Here again, without effective facilitation of said experiences and activities, they do not become, in Dewey's words, "educative."

In the summer of 2012, I co-led a faculty development workshop experience in the Uinta Wilderness area of Utah. This ten-day backpacking expedition was designed to introduce faculty to the theories and practices of experiential education in the college context. As my co-leader and I planned this program, it became clear to both of us that the best way to design this workshop was to give participants the opportunity to actually experience experiential education. It would not be enough to sit in a classroom somewhere for the week, and simply read and talk about it. We knew that having participants move through the processes of experiential education while learning about it would be crucial.

Our group of ten faculty members ran the gamut from biology and chemistry to political science and education. We flew into Salt Lake City and spent the night in town getting to know each other and going over course goals and group expectations. The next day, we drove out to trailhead and began our hike, making sure to cover fewer miles than we might otherwise to let folks acclimatize and get used to carrying 50-plus pounds on their backs for mile after mile. Each afternoon, we arrived in camp, set up, and scheduled free-time for people to relax and get settled. After an early dinner, we would gather and discuss the topic for the day—sometimes it was a reading on teaching and learning issues in higher education, sometimes it was something specific on experiential education, and sometimes it was just a chance to discuss what happened that day on trail or anything else that happened to be on folks' minds. The discussions were led by either myself or my co-leader although, in actuality, it took little more than a prompt or two to get the conversation started and perhaps a nudge along the way to keep the discussion on track. We kept up this routine for the next eight days as we traveled throughout the high alpine meadows and ridgelines of the Uinta Mountains.

On the last night in the woods, we reserved a time for participants to talk about their biggest takeaways from the experience. A dominant theme emerged from this discussion—an appreciation for the importance of facilitation in experiential learning. Whether it was tone setting and framing of the experience as a whole, thoughtful prompts during group discussions, adjustments to the itinerary or schedule based on feedback, or mediation of (relatively minor) group conflict, this group of college professors "got it" that facilitation knowledge, skills, and abilities were a crucial part of effective experiential education. And, as my co-leader and I suspected, the only real way they were able to "get it" was by actively experiencing it—and we certainly wanted to practice what we preached!

But, importantly, the group remained a little unclear on the specific methods and mechanics of effective facilitation. It was a bit like a "secret sauce" to them. They knew it when they saw it and experienced it, but they were not entirely clear how to go about doing it themselves in experiential contexts. For some, especially our science colleagues, the idea of an open-ended hour of "group discussion" with no direction was borderline terrifying. Others struggled to feel confident that they could manage group development and interpersonal conflict were it to arise in their classrooms. After all, they were trained as scholars, not as student life personnel. While it is true that a lot of good facilitation can be hard to boil down to hard-and-fast rules, there are some fundamentals within the context of experiential education that every college teacher can grasp. In this chapter, we will first explore the concept of facilitation—what it is and why it matters in experiential education. Then we will discuss four critical areas of effective facilitation—tone setting, processing, differentiation, and group dynamics.

FACILITATION: HAVING EYES TO SEE

What do we mean in experiential education when we talk about "facilitation"? The word comes from the French *facile,* which roughly means "easy." At its most basic, facilitation means to help "make easy" the learning in a given educational context. Most of us intuitively understand what that looks like in a typical college classroom. We facilitate learning every day through well-designed classroom plans—whether through direct instruction, group projects, or general class discussion. We also facilitate in smaller ways by intervening as needed when a small group discussion goes off-topic, when a student is chronically late, or when the entire class fails the mid-term. In each of these cases we are actively reading and reacting to what we see in front of us in the classroom. But it is important to recognize that good classroom facilitation doesn't happen automatically. A glance at most new college instructors will reveal a host of facilitation inadequacies and mistakes. Indeed, as I think back on my first years as a college teacher, I cringe at what I did and did not do in terms of "making easy" classroom activity and learning.

In any educational environment, a teacher has to have the "eyes to see"—that is, they must be a reflective practitioner in the way Schon (1983) articulated: as "a dialogue between thinking and doing through which [the teacher] becomes more skillful" (p. 31). In order to facilitate, to make easy, a teacher must first be able to see and "read" educational processes through a dialogue between thinking and doing. Do you have the "eyes to see" that the same group of students sits in the back, unengaged? Or that several students are dominating discussion? Or that you have assigned way too much reading and students have resorted to skipping it entirely since you aren't covering it in class anyway? In my work with younger, pre-tenure faculty, one of the biggest developmental hurdles in their teaching is simply having the diagnostic "eyes to see" what is happening in their classrooms and with their students. It is a necessary prerequisite to effective facilitation. Experienced (and talented) teachers often do this so intuitively that they have a hard time explaining why they do what they do—they just know that, in that moment, they needed to do it. Malcolm Gladwell refers to this skill as "thin-slicing." To Gladwell, experts have a remarkable ability to process information for sophisticated judgment in a short period of time. This runs counter to the more accepted notion that the more one thinks about something, the better the judgment. As Gladwell points out using the analogy of a birdwatcher:

> When it comes down to being in the field and looking at the bird, you don't take time to analyze it and say it shows this, this, and this; therefore it must be this species. It's more natural and instinctive. After a lot of practice, you look at the bird, and it triggers little switches in your brain. It *looks* right. You know what it is at a glance.
>
> (2007, p. 45)

Experienced teachers, like experienced birders, also do this. They can "thin-slice" educational process and recognize what needs to be done in a relatively quick period of time whereas a newer, less experienced teacher does not have the same "eyes to see"—the classroom has no pattern, no noticeable places to intervene—it just looks like a jumble.

As we move from traditional classroom contexts to experiential ones, this process is the same. It takes time to have the "eyes to see" what needs to be done to facilitate effective experiential learning. And the need for effective facilitation is amplified in experiential contexts. Why? As we have discussed throughout this book, experiential processes move the learning paradigm from a relatively static and controlled one-way knowledge transmission to more dynamic, interactive, and less controlled knowledge co-creation. Once we move, literally and figuratively, out from behind the lectern, we enter into Palmer's domain of the "live encounter." We know pretty much what will happen in a tightly organized lecture-oriented class (even if we pepper it with a few small group discussions and the like). But once we open up the educational space to a sense of co-created learning, we can't really anticipate or predict what will happen. Including a service learning component into your syllabus, an in-depth simulation in your class, or an authentic project-based

110

assignment into your course leaves quite a bit "undetermined." Science faculty understand, for example, that well-designed labs can yield mistakes, surprises, and serendipitous occurrences that can amplify the learning, but only if these occurrences are capitalized on by "marking" those moments for students as educative. And this requires facilitation. But, you might ask, how does one develop this facilitative skill, the "eyes to see" in experiential processes, without simply resorting to the "school of hard knocks" approach? While gaining experience is important, there are four key concepts that can help move a teacher along into more effective facilitation of experiential learning: tone setting, processing, differentiation, and group dynamics.

TONE SETTING

All effective teachers know that a classroom culture that is not grounded in trust, acceptance, and appropriate risk-taking is a classroom unprepared to take full advantage of learning. How do you create such a culture whether in a classroom or on some out-of-class extended experience? You must commit time and energy to it. This can be difficult when we feel pulled back toward the "Primacy of Content" teaching paradigm discussed in Chapter 4. Consider the analogy of the bow and arrow. To shoot an arrow you spend almost all your time and effort pulling backward, in the opposite direction you want the arrow to go. Rush that process or neglect it and your outcome (arrow flight distance) will be disappointing. But invest the appropriate time and energy into "pulling back the arrow" and it will likely yield huge benefits when it comes time to let go. Building relationships and classroom culture early in an experience both student-to-teacher and student-to-student is the equivalent of pulling back the arrow. It may seem the opposite of where you want to go but that investment will allow you to launch the learning when it comes time to process the experiences.

My college has run an outdoor orientation program (August Wilderness) for in-coming students since 1971. In the early part of my career here at Earlham, I was responsible for directing this program and training student and faculty leaders for this experience. I would get the unique perspective of seeing the groups on campus before they left and then seeing them three weeks later when they returned. The "time-lapse" images of these groups were always fascinating. The groups that returned were completely different and virtually unrecognizable from the groups that departed. While all the returning groups were gregarious and free-spirited with each other (not to mention quite a bit smellier), it was also interesting to see the differences in the groups. Some were much tighter, closer, and more supportive than others. What happened in those three weeks to create these different kinds of outcomes? Over the years, as I listened to instructors during the post-program review meetings, a pattern clearly emerged. The groups that were the most functional, socially, were the ones where the instructors spent a conscious effort on what I now describe as "tone setting." The groups that were less functional and successful realized (too late) that they missed this crucial component of effective experiential facilitation. What do we mean by "tone setting"? Tone refers to how an instructor both models and frames positive and effective group behavior and interaction. Some basics of tone setting include:

1. Allocating adequate time for the formation of personal and group goals.
2. Facilitating a consensus-oriented discussion (or series of discussions depending on the length of the experience) on ground rules and individual as well as community expectations.
3. Structured feedback mechanisms on what is working and what can be improved (both instructor-to-student and student-to-student).
4. Overt attention to "group norms" that celebrate the importance of both commonalities and differences.
5. Acceptance of "healthy" conflict as well as strategies, structures, and methods for conflict resolution.

We read a lot in the literature on teaching and learning that it is important to create a safe atmosphere in the classroom. However, sometimes that notion can become twisted around to mean "no risks." In fact, most of us want appropriate risk-taking in our students and most learning involves some degree of risk and "discomfort" as we already discussed. I cannot guarantee that my students will feel "safe" in my class or in a given learning situation if by safe we mean "comfortable." But I can and should guarantee that I will monitor activity and the group to ensure we are empathetic, caring, respectful, and appropriate in terms of the risks we take with each other. And this kind of tone setting is especially critical when dealing with emotionally charged topics and issues. As Crowley notes:

> I teach some grim stuff. I teach a lot about oppression and identity and yet my classrooms mostly are joyful spaces—students want to be there and they feel fully present . . . There is a direct relationship between building demo-cratic community for hard dialogue and people feeling very connected to one another. This really happens through experiential education. I couldn't do the

work I do pressing students to think hard at a white majority institution about something like race if they weren't connected to one another and to me. It's too easy to dehumanize someone in those difficult conversations.

(Personal communication, 2015)

Asking students themselves to develop "ground rules" for the experience can help to build the democratic community that Crowley speaks of here. In experiential education contexts, this is sometimes referred to as a "full-value contract"—that is, how can we, as a community, get "full value" out of the learning? At the start of the semester (or experience), I often asked students to make a list of "what works" in discussion and reflection activities and what doesn't. They are usually quite good at bringing out the usual suspects—come prepared, don't hog discussion time, be respectful, be rigorous, don't just look to the teacher to ask questions, etc. This list then becomes something everyone is held accountable to (including me as the instructor). It is important that this not be a one-off "event" but rather a living, breathing document that "has a seat at the table," so to speak in every class. Think about creating certain "catch phrases" or even physical motions that help keep the group on track. For example, one year, my students used the "reel it in" fishing motion if they felt that the discussion was off topic. In another group, we all agreed to avoid sarcastic comments—calling them "zingers" and labeling them when folks failed to live up to the agreed upon group standards. When students start calling each other out (and you) on such group norms you know you have created a culture and the appropriate conditions necessary for effective processing.

While the examples above may appear to apply most directly to small-scale seminars and group experiences, tone-setting is also critical in large-scale classrooms as well. Even in a lecture hall filled with 125 students, you can still consciously focus on tone setting. Polling students on what works and doesn't work in large, lecture-style classrooms is just as relevant as in small seminars. Students can easily point out the things that bug them in larger classes—the instructor lecturing too fast and not pausing for questions, students arriving late, leaving during the middle, checking Facebook or the cellphone during class, etc. You can work on building relationships with students: I ask students in my larger classes to complete a "student questionnaire" and attach a photo so that I can get to know them better. In the questionnaire, I ask them about what other classes they are taking that semester, about their interests outside class, and about their "hopes and fears" for the course. Using small group break-outs and "think-pair-shares" in larger classes sets the tone that, even in large, fixed seat lecture halls we can build community with each other. Using clickers, twitter feeds, and online forums can also help with tone setting, and can be done more efficiently than general group discussion. I have found that students are more willing to participate in large classes when these kinds of structures are created. Regardless of the size of the class or group, or the context of the learning (inside or outside the classroom), tone setting is an essential part of effective facilitation in experiential education. Get the tone wrong and everything becomes harder—like a negative feedback loop. Get it right, and it tends to reinforce itself—making your job as a facilitator that much easier.

PROCESSING

The concept of processing in facilitation refers to the ways in which a teacher encourages active reflection throughout an educational experience. This is, to many experiential educators, the single most important principle to ensure that learning actually happens from experience. As we have discussed, for Dewey, processing was the key distinguishing element that moves something from "primary" or direct experience to "secondary" or educative experience. Other terms are often used to signify processing, including "reflection," "guided inquiry," and "debriefing." I have chosen to use the term "processing" as I believe that it is the best signifier of the facilitative principle at hand. "Reflection" can sometimes imply that it is something we only do after an experience and that, as we will discover, is not always the case. We are constantly thinking and processing throughout an experience. "Guided inquiry" seems apt but perhaps signifies that a learner must be guided through learning by the teacher, which is often true but not universally so. "Debriefing" seems to be a somewhat awkward term (conjuring up embarrassing middle-school memories). So, what then is "processing" in experiential education? Luckner and Nadler define it as "an activity that is structured to encourage individuals to plan, reflect, describe, analyze, and communicate about experiences" (1997, p. 8). And, importantly, processing can happen throughout experiential activity—before, during, and after.

Processing does a number of important things in experiential education. First, it allows individuals to focus on the situation or learning at hand prior to an activity or experience (this is part of "framing" as described in the previous chapter). Second, it can allow individuals or groups to adjust their behavior or thinking during an experience. Third, it can help individuals and groups to "mark" significant learning following an experiential activity. Finally, processing can facilitate the transfer of learning to new or novel contexts (Gass, 1993; Luckner & Nadler, 1997). If we review the basic experiential learning cycle introduced in Chapter 2 and adjust for this notion of processing happening throughout, it now looks like this:

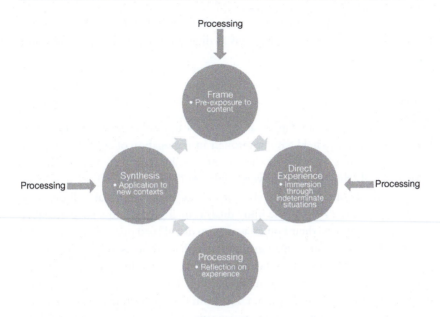

FIGURE 6.1 Processing within the experiential learning cycle

As Caine and Caine (1991) state: "active processing is not just a stage in a lesson. It does not occur at one specific time, nor is it something that can be done in only one way. It is a matter of constantly 'working' and 'kneading' the ongoing experience that students have" (p. 157).

The importance of processing is strongly supported in the literature on teaching and learning—particularly as we know more about the neuroscience of learning. Studies have demonstrated the importance of active processing in pattern making, memory, and neural connectivity (Campbell, 1989; Dozier, 1992; Jensen, 2000). And Bransford et al. (2000) note in regards to the importance of metacognition:

Teaching practices congruent with a metacognitive approach to learning include those that focus on sense-making, self-assessment, and reflection on what worked and what needs improving. These practices have been shown to increase the degree to which students transfer their learning to new settings and events.

(p. 12)

It is clear that processing is a critical facilitative skill in experiential education, that it happens throughout the learning activity, and that it supports student learning. But we are still left with what, specifically, processing looks like in experiential education and how it is done. It is helpful, I think, to see processing as something that happens at different *scales*, in distinct *forms*, and with varying *methods*.

Scales

To begin, processing can happen at different scales, either related to a discrete experience (such as a field trip) or through an aggregation of experiences (such as a semester-long course). At the largest possible aggregated scale for our purposes in higher education, you could even think about how a student processes their four-year experience at college or in their major. Processing also happens at the level of the individual, a small group, and a large group. A student might process their homestay experience abroad one way, for example, but after discussing it in a small group with fellow students, might change her perspective as she listens to her peers. What is the functional difference between "small" and "large" group processing? There is no hard-and-fast rule here, but I often find small groups range from two to 16 individuals. Anything over that becomes "large group" processing. Large group processing could mean a "class discussion" with 35 students or it could theoretically involve an online course of well over 1,000 students with virtual interaction taking place on discussion boards, etc. The point here is to remember that processing is not simply something that happens during a discrete experience (although it can). To effectively facilitate experiential education, you must be mindful of how you are processing the experience and at what scale.

Forms and Methods

In addition to scale, there are also a variety of forms processing can take including (but certainly not limited to):

1.   group discussion (either in-person or virtual);
2.   journaling and other writing forms and prompts;
3.   one-on-one meetings;
4.   digital platforms (e-portfolios, blogs, videos, etc.);
5.   oral presentations.

There are many methods within these forms that can also be employed. For example, group discussions need not always be done the same way. It is common for experiential educators to mix up processing methods in group discussion such that sometimes it might involve small groups, sometimes the whole group, sometimes pairs or trios, and sometimes asynchronously through online forums and discussion posts. One very effective technique I have used to mix up class discussion in somewhat larger classes (35–70) is the "fishbowl." Students are divided into a smaller "inside" discussion subgroup (approximately four–eight) and a larger "outside" group. A topic or question is introduced to the inside group for discussion. Members of the outside group are asked to listen closely and formulate responses and/or questions to what they are hearing but are not (at this point) permitted to speak. After some time, the facilitator pauses the inside discussion and asks for responses or questions from the outside group back into the inside group. After a suitable time-frame of exchange, the inside group adjourns to the outside group and a new inside subgroup is formed with a new topic. Other effective methods to vary discussion include the "world café" structure and the cooperative jigsaw.[1]

Processing as Fire Starting

Regardless of the scale, method, or form, effective processing has several common features and structures. Consider processing like starting a fire. You need four things: appropriate conditions, good kindling, a spark, and oxygen. The following visual model identifies the major components of effective processing.

Each of these elements depends upon the other. You cannot start a fire without a spark and you cannot keep a fire going without appropriate levels of oxygen. It requires all the elements working together in concert to maintain a healthy fire.

To begin, effective facilitation of individual and group processing requires attention to the establishment of appropriate conditions. To return to our fire analogy, if we give inadequate attention to setting up appropriate conditions for processing, we have little chance of creating educative experience—it would be like trying to start a fire out in the open in the pouring rain. Pearson and Smith (1985), identify several factors that are important to setting the appropriate conditions for processing:

1. committing to its importance and central role in experience-based learning;
2. deliberately planning for an adequate opportunity to reflect;
3. realizing that a high level of facilitation skill is needed;
4. establishing clear intentions, objectives, and purposes for all activities; . . .

117

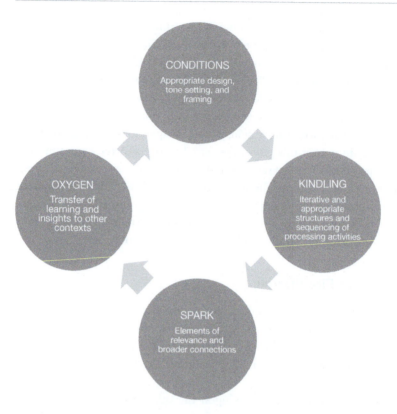

FIGURE 6.2 Processing and the fire analogy

5. establishing an environment based upon trust, acceptance, risk taking, and mutual respect of individuals' feelings, perceptions, and theories.

(Quoted in Knapp, pp. 35–36)

Much of what we have already explored in the facilitative skill of "tone setting" applies here. It is worth noting, however, the central importance of providing adequate time for processing. Too often, processing is cut short because we just had to cram in one more content piece, or one more activity. I recall an example of a faculty member planning a May term to Europe where he had planned for the group to visit something like seven countries in three weeks. When I looked at his itinerary and asked him when the group would have time to actually process the experiences they were having he gave me a funny look and replied, "on the train?" After more thinking, he scaled back his itinerary substantially and included "reflection days" interspersed between significant experiences. The end result was not only much less hectic on him as a facilitator/leader, it was more educative for his students.

Once we have created the appropriate conditions for processing, we need good "kindling" to allow the fire to catch. When I try to help newer instructors learn how to carry a good class discussion or reflection, I often find that one of the most basic errors is a failure to start with "kindling." What normally happens is an attempt to dump a "big log" on the fire and hope it catches. For example, let's say students have just experienced a field trip to Kapiti Island, a conservation reserve for native birds off the north island of New Zealand, as part of their off-campus semester in environmental studies. The faculty leader, full of excitement and enthusiasm, starts off the reflection session by asking students the following: "now, as you all know from the reading we did about the social construction of nature, how was this particular experience an example of the authors' central thesis?" Silence. The question is both too vague and too big of a log. Students aren't "there" yet. The discussion facilitator needed to start with smaller sticks first to get them going. A common technique here is the "What? So what? Now what?" frame. Start students off by simply asking open-ended questions about what they observed, what happened, etc. Let them collectively process the activity or event themselves. As this happens, listen carefully for patterns, themes, or connections that can be made. Then, you might begin following up with specific things you noticed. "Jane," the faculty leader asks, "I noticed that you said you didn't like seeing the tags on the birds feet on the island. What about that bothered you?" Jane replies and the leader might then redirect the question to the whole group—"Did anyone else feel the same and, if so, why? If not, why not?"

At some point, the leader needs to then walk the processing into the "So what?" phase, marking the experience as significant. Returning again to our fire analogy, the "So what?" phase provides the "spark"—that creative element that really moves processing from the simple act of telling and retelling to the more profound space of learning. In my experience, this is really the key phase of processing. Too much reflection in experiential education stays at the surface— the "What?" phase, without making the more rigorous connections between theory and practice. There is no spark. No fire. Whether it is reading a vacuous journal entry on what a student did on their internship, or holding a discussion after a simulation that was "fun" but seemingly not terribly educative, there are few things less enjoyable than "rote" reflection. This is what Freire was referring to as "idle chatter" in the quotation that begins this chapter. Learn to see it and then work hard to ensure that your students don't fall into that habit.

Returning to our Kapiti Island example, the faculty leader knows these traps and chimes in as students talk through what they experienced on the island: "So, it sounds like many of us felt like there was some sense of 'wildness' or 'self determination' lost among the species on this island with the creation of the reserve. Some of us even compared Kapiti to a giant zoo! What do you think our author would have to say about that?" If you are not facilitating a discussion but asking students to process in writing, or in some other form, you might need to make this move from shallow to deeper processing more overt through structured assignments and prompts. In some of my own written reflection assignments, I try to make clear the distinctions between different modes of reflective writing (descriptive, analytical, integrative), provide examples of each, and design rubrics that assess the degree to which students demonstrate each mode. Good "prompts" in written reflection assignments are as important as good questions in group discussions (Bean, 2011). They are cut from the same facilitative cloth. Ask "bad" writing prompts and you'll get bad reflection.

The final element of our fire is the "So what?" phase (the "oxygen") where you ask students to integrate key learning and realizations to other contexts outside the immediate experience. This provides the necessary energy to keep the fire going beyond the initial spark—like blowing on embers. As the discussion about the Kapiti Island experience continues, the faculty leader may ask: "I wonder, what really is the difference between a zoo and a wild place? Is our planet, at this point, so managed, so developed, that nothing can really be called 'natural' any more? And, does that mean that conservation areas such as Kapiti are really just for our own benefit? To assuage our own sense of guilt?" This is a "big log" prompt but by this point the fire has been properly prepared for its inclusion. As students wrestle with this question, they bring up other experiences on the New Zealand program, other perspectives from their disciplines (biology, philosophy, sociology) and work through how to place this Kapiti experience in context. The instructor knows, at this point, drawing from an old Quaker phrase, to "not speak, unless you can improve upon the silence." Too much interjection from the teacher at this point can serve as a dampening element on your fire. Remember, teaching is listening and learning is talking. In general, when facilitating, you will want to keep most of your questions open-ended and exploratory. Paul and Binker (1990) list six categories of questions that are useful to consider in processing experiences:

1. questions of clarification (e.g., "what do you mean by . . . ?");
2. questions that probe assumptions (e.g., "What is Daren assuming?");
3. questions that probe reasons and evidence (e.g., "Why do you think that is true?");
4. questions about viewpoints of perspectives (e.g., "Why have you chosen this rather than that perspective?");

5. questions that probe implications and consequences (e.g., "What effect would that have?"); and

6. questions about the question (e.g., "How can we find out?").

(Quoted in Knapp, p. 62)

Montessori teachers are trained to use the phrase "I wonder . . .?" when asking questions. Try it out. I have found it a very effective way to pose questions in a more invitational way. Finally, make sure to be attentive to balancing voices in the group. There can be nothing more frustrating for students than hearing from the classroom "loud mouth" ad nauseum. If you have set the tone from the beginning, your students will call each other out on this. If not, make sure to revisit the agreed upon ground rules to ensure a respectful and inclusive atmosphere.

While the example used with Kapiti Island is one where the processing happens after the experience, remember that this is not the only place that processing can happen. In fact, how that Kapiti Island field trip was initially framed is, in a sense, processing the experience, along with any peer or instructor interjections along the way. Facilitating processing along like this takes some practice but the key point is to start small, with "kindling," listen attentively, and find ways to add bigger "logs" to the fire to connect the experience to learning. One practical frame to keep in mind is Eyler at al. (1997) "four c's of reflection." These are an excellent mnemonic for effective processing in experiential contexts.

1. **Continuous** in time-frame. Make sure reflection is a process—not just a singular event.

2. **Connected** to intellectual and academic needs. Purposefully connect processing to educational outcomes through evaluation and specified criteria.

3. **Challenging** to assumptions and complacency. Make sure to create an environment where processing is rigorous and respected (as opposed to vacuous and rote). Have students hold each other accountable.

4. **Contextualized** in design and setting. Work hard to design and frame the experience well and "build your fire" to set up for meaningful and in-depth processing.

DIFFERENTIATION

I often do an exercise with my students to illustrate the concept of differentiation in effective facilitation of experiential processes.[2] We begin by clustering together in a tight group with foam balls in our hands. I instruct students to throw the balls directly above their heads and, if they feel the need, to move out of the way if they would like. In this round, almost all students throw the balls in the air and stay in place because they are not particularly worried about the consequences of a foam ball landing on their heads. We might view this as their "comfort zone." In the next round, I introduce tennis balls and ask students to do the same thing. This time, a few people either wince, duck, or even move out of the way. The consequences of a tennis ball, while not extreme, have upped the ante on the group. After this round, the students have a sense that things are going to get tougher. This is when I bring out the box of water balloons (I do this outside). As the group throws the balloons in the air, the reaction is interesting—some "risk-taker" students love it and stay right where they are—enjoying the rush of the unknown. Others bolt immediately, not wanting to risk getting wet. After this round I announce one final round and the students look at me wondering whether or not I will be bringing out knives, lawn darts, or some such thing. I bring out a new box of water balloons but this time I tell them that the balloons are filled with the cheapest department store perfume I could find (this is not true but they don't know that for sure). As the students throw the balloons in the air, nearly everyone bolts except the one or two students who enjoy being contrarian. In the discussion that follows, I ask students to talk about where their "limit" was— the point at which they were unwilling to participate any longer. Two things always seem to come from this—first, there is variability among the group as to what is enough of a "risk" and, second, that the perception of risk is somewhat socially mediated (what we might think of typically as peer pressure). Most teachers are familiar here with the notion of the "comfort zone." In experiential education, this is a crucial facilitative framework. Drawn from the Yerkes–Dodson (1908) law of Optimal Arousal, Vgotsky's (1978) Zone of Proximal Development, and Csikszentmihalyi's (1997) "flow" theory, the comfort zone framework argues that there are zones of learning that produce different responses among learners. Too much perceived risk or challenge to a student will not produce an educative state (the "panic" zone, so to speak). Conversely, too little risk or challenge may keep a student from learning at all (the "comfort" zone). What we are after, ideally, is for each one of our students to be in between both comfort and panic in what some have termed the "learning zone."

What does all this mean for facilitating experiential education? The principle of differentiation means both designing and monitoring experiential activity for maximum challenge and engagement—avoiding too much comfort and too much perceived "threat." This can show up in a whole host of ways. I have facilitated classroom simulations that became too heated or personal in terms of the classroom interactions and I needed to adjust or intervene to keep the right level of challenge and engagement for the class as a whole. An internship opportunity could be viewed as being too low on challenge (minor clerical work, for example) or too high (having too much responsibility without adequate support). Off-campus study opportunities are common places where students can experience both educative challenges and (sometimes) mis-educative threat. And, here again, students on the same program, having the same experiences, may react quite differently. To some students, a homestay on Maasai tribal lands in Tanzania is the opportunity of a lifetime; to others, it is an overwhelming experience. The facilitative skill, here, is to determine when to push students and how far. To differentiate, in this manner, means to constantly monitor and adjust the learning to enhance "educative experience." As Dewey (1938) argued: "A primary responsibility of educators is that they not only be aware of the general principle of the shaping of actual experience by environing conditions, but that they also recognize in the concrete what surroundings are conducive to having experiences that lead to growth" (p. 40). A community-based learning project, for example, for which students are unprepared and not given sufficient time will not be educative. Conversely, a community-based activity that is too simplistic, easy, or disintegrated from academic content would also fail. But, through effective facilitation, almost *any* experience can be made to be educative. What it takes is monitoring and adjustment to ensure that students are in that "learning zone." Csikszentmihalyi (1997) identifies several key components that lead to such flow experiences: "1) A clear set of goals; 2) high levels of feedback; and, 3) challenges that are just above manageable relative to skill set" (p. 30). This is what we mean by differentiation. You cannot just design the experience and let it run its course. An effective experiential educator is constantly monitoring activities to ensure proper differentiation—both looking at each individual and at the group as a whole. This requires being present with your students in both big and small ways, and again, having the "eyes to see." Here are some suggested ways you can "thin-slice" experiential learning activities to monitor and adjust for differentiation:

1. Design iterative feedback into the process. I often use Covey's (1992) "continue, start, stop" frame. What should we continue to do? What should we start doing? What should we stop doing?
2. Work your group "inside-out." Check in with individual students throughout to monitor their engagement and perceived level of challenge.

123

3. Work your group "outside-in." I often try to "feel the room" or "feel the group." As social creatures, we humans have a strong intuitive sense of group mood. Does the group seem energized? Stressed? Tired? Make a conscious effort to read your group and make adjustments.

4. Plan for differentiation. Make sure there is flexibility in your design to allow for some students to "up-shift" into more challenge and for other students, if appropriate, to "down-shift."

5. Balance ritual and novelty. A general rule of thumb is to have approximately 60 percent of what you do together to be ritualized—traditions, patterns, or constants that help students anchor themselves in what is expected in the learning environment. The remaining 40 percent should be "novel." Novelty in facilitation is simply anything that breaks patterns—through intrigue, playfulness, surprise, or other creative forms of expression. Too much ritual can be boring. Too much novelty may be too overwhelming or over-stimulating.

GROUP DYNAMICS

While some experiential education is individually oriented (such as an internship experience), a far greater percentage involves some form of group interaction and "social learning." A central tenet in experiential education, and progressive education more generally, is that the social dynamics of learning are a fundamental component of the learning process as well as what it means to be "well educated" (Dewey, 1958; Johnson & Johnson, 1989; Noddings, 2005; Vgotsky, 1978). Most college and university instructors would agree with this line of reasoning. And yet, we tend to spend surprisingly little time actively facilitating social learning and development in our classrooms. As students transition from college to career, the vast majority of them will be expected to work cooperatively and collaboratively with other people. They must be able to demonstrate both leadership and followership. They must be able to work across differences and disagreements. All these sorts of "team" behaviors and skills deserve attention in the 21st-century college classroom, yet why do we so often ignore this part of student development? Mostly, because it takes time; it is perceived as "non-academic," and we are poorly trained as facilitators of group dynamics. But, as we have discussed throughout this book, experiential education asks us to take a hard look at the outcomes and results of "content-heavy" direct instruction and to move from the paradigm of teaching to student learning. When we do this, it becomes increasingly clear that we ought to place more emphasis on the social dynamics of learning than we do. In experiential education, this is particularly important. As we have discussed, we don't want students to come away from an experiential project with the idea that hell is other people. To avoid this, experiential educators need to understand several elements that go into effective facilitation of groups including an understanding of group development theory and strategies for conflict resolution.

THEORIES OF GROUP DEVELOPMENT

To help groups effectively move through experiential learning processes, both the instructor and the students should be aware of the basics of group development. Tuckman (1965) is most commonly cited in experiential education as it relates to models of group development. Tuckman's five stages include: forming, storming, norming, performing, and adjourning. The model suggests that groups move through each "phase" as they work together. In the "forming" stage, groups are on their best behavior, tend to communicate at a more surface level, and focus on the basics (Who am I in this group? Who is in this group with me? What is the task?). In the "storming" phase, groups leave the "honeymoon" stage as conflict tends to arise around group norms, expectations, roles, and personalities. The "norming" phase ostensibly moves groups past basic disagreements about roles and expectations as the group norms to some commonly accepted rules and agreements. In the "performing" phase, the group is able to function at a high task level as the team clicks into well-defined roles and effective interactions. Finally, the "adjourning" phase brings the group full-circle as individuals begin to think about and consider both the conclusion of the work and the transition to other tasks or contexts. While this is a solid basic description of group development, it is important to point out that groups are rarely so sequential in their development. Napier and Gershenfeld (1981), for example, argued:

> Although . . . there do appear to be rather clear patterns of development [in groups], it would be unwise to take them too seriously. Each group, like each individual, is unique and must be understood in terms of exceptions, and in terms of when, how, and why changes in development occur.
>
> (p. 447)

In reality, groups are much more organic than a simple lock-step sequence of stages and often move in between these stages at varying points throughout a common experience. That being said, there are elements of practical truth

125

in these so-called stages in my experience working with groups. As Napier and Gershenfeld note: "[n]evertheless, it appears that group development is on many occasions more predictable than individual behavior" (p. 447).

Most teaching faculty will recognize the basic elements of group dynamics and development described here. Classes (at least relatively small ones) usually exhibit many of these characteristics of forming, storming, norming, performing, and adjourning. In experiential education facilitation, it is important to recognize, as an instructor, what kind of support is needed during each of these categories or phases. There will be times when you need to be more directive and prescriptive while at others you should be more hands-off or alongside. Even better, spending time *with* your class in explaining these elements of group dynamics can help students help themselves—recognizing when they are "storming," for example, and what they need to do to move through it. And this leads us to another element of effective facilitation of group dynamics—conflict resolution strategies.

CONFLICT RESOLUTION STRATEGIES

The first thing I do when group conflict arises in experiential contexts is to remind myself that it is an important part of the learning and the process. In almost all my best experiences with experiential education, conflict played a significant role. If there is no group conflict, or some challenge or obstacle to overcome, it could be argued that the project or experience was not designed properly. The point, in experiential facilitation, is not to avoid conflict but rather to effectively identify it and help the group move through it. One helpful model I have found in this process is the Waterline Model.

In this model, any given group, while working through a task, may experience conflict. While the conflict may be visible "above the surface" such as with arguing, dysfunctional work outputs, etc., the conflict often has deeper issues below the surface that a facilitator should be on the look-out for. The maintenance response of the facilitator depends on his or her read of how "deep" the conflict goes. Some conflict, for example, can be traced back to issues with the structure of the task (goals and roles), while others can be traced to issues within the group (what we discussed above in relationship to developmental stages). These two areas tend to be the easiest to address and help the group move through from a facilitator's point of view. In the model, they are closer to the waterline, so to speak. Conflict can also arise interpersonally—between two or more people who just rub each other the wrong way or with identity issues (race, gender, social class, etc.). Or you can have conflict at the intrapersonal level—one individual who, for any number

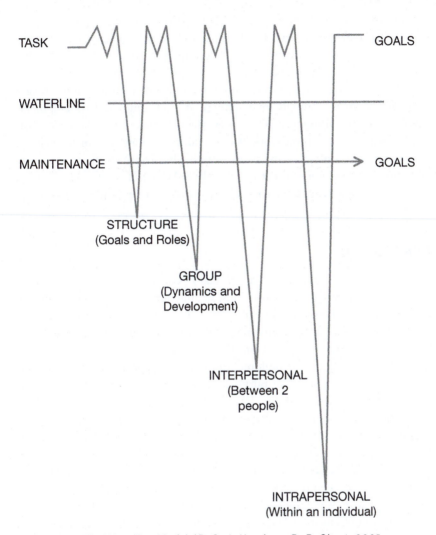

TASK

WATERLINE

MAINTENANCE

GOALS

GOALS

STRUCTURE
(Goals and Roles)

GROUP
(Dynamics and
Development)

INTERPERSONAL
(Between 2
people)

INTRAPERSONAL
(Within an individual)

FIGURE 6.3 The Waterline Model (R. S. J. Harrison, R. R. Short, 2001. Waterline Model of Diagnostic and Therapeutic Intervention. Kenmore, WA: Leadership Institute of Seattle)

of reasons, appears to be at the center of the problem. These last two areas tend to be more difficult to resolve from a facilitator's point of view— explaining why in the model they are depicted "deeper" below the surface. Often, inter- or intrapersonal conflict involves levels of personality and psychology that your typical instructor is not necessarily well trained to work with. That, or the time necessary to get at the issues in sufficient depth is just

127

not possible. The good news is that the large percentage of group conflict for your average experiential venture is located nearer to the surface in either issues with the structure or issues with the group. The main takeaway of the Waterline Model in terms of conflict resolution is to recognize that instructors have the ability to facilitate groups through conflict by focusing on the basics of goals and roles (through tone setting), and dynamics and development (through situational support). This covers the vast majority of the issues that arise in experiential group work. We should not shy away from facilitating group work and conflict in educational settings. In fact, we should create more educational opportunities for it to take place. As one of my favorite faculty colleagues at Earlham used to say, "we need to help students be more comfortable being uncomfortable."

CONCLUSION

Experiential education is a facilitation-heavy pedagogy. To allow experiences to become "educative," instructors must be fully present in ways we often do not have to be in a more traditional college classroom. We give fewer answers and ask more questions. We focus on creating structures for student engagement and less on Powerpoint slides. We practice the skills of intervention, redirection, and mediation. We design multiple and iterative opportunities for student reflection and processing. We purposefully incorporate flexibility and open spaces into the syllabus and pay close attention in order to make adjustments along the way. I began this chapter using the analogy of the payload and propulsion system of a rocket in order to describe the importance of facilitation. But there is another way to view the principles we have explored here. I recently attended the holiday concert of our college orchestra. In the auditorium, I watched the conductor walk on stage, tap her baton, and begin the performance. Watching her, I realized that what she was doing was the embodiment of facilitation. She helped the orchestra "tune up"—what we have described here in the importance of tone setting and framing. Without proper preparation and tuning, the music will never reach its potential. Throughout the performance, the ensemble is processing information, adjusting to each other as they try to perform at the highest level they can. The conductor is also listening attentively to the various instruments, asking some to speed up, others to quiet down—what we have discussed here as differentiation. When it works, it is a beautiful thing to behold. The conductor matters, and matters hugely, but she also is but one piece in the ensemble—and she allows the musicians to shine through in how she orchestrates the experience. If I have learned anything in experiential education these last 20 years, it is that facilitation is both a science (the rocket ship) and an art (the conductor). We do know some things about how to make it work and work well. I also know, from experience, that simple rule following will only get you so far. But if you can cultivate the "eyes to see" in educational process, you will set yourself up to constantly work on the craft. This is, perhaps, the most important facilitative lesson of all.

NOTES

1. See www.theworldcafe.com for more information on World Café facilitation protocols and www.jigsaw.org for more on the cooperative jigsaw method.
2. Special thanks to Christian Bisson, Associate Professor of Adventure Education at Plymouth State University, for this exercise.

REFERENCES

Bean, J. C. (2011). *Engaging Ideas: The Professor's Guide to Integrating Writing, Critical Thinking, and Active Learning in the Classroom*. New York: John Wiley & Sons.

Bransford, J., Brown, A., Cocking, R., Donovan, S., & Pellegrino, J. (2000). *How People Learn: Brain, Mind, Experience, and School*. Washington, DC: National Academy Press.

Caine, R. N., & Caine, G. (1991). *Making Connections: Teaching and the Human Brain*. Alexandria, VA: Association for Supervision and Curriculum Development.

Campbell, J. (1989). *The Improbable Machine: What the Upheavals in Artificial Intelligence Research Reveal About How the Mind Really Works*. New York: Simon & Schuster.

Covey, S. R. (1992). *Principle Centered Leadership*. New York: Simon & Schuster.

Crowley, K. (2015). Personal communication.

Csikszentmihalyi, M. (1997). *Finding Flow: The Psychology of Engagement with Everyday Life*. New York: Basic Books.

Dewey, J. (1958). *Experience and Nature*. New York: Courier Dover Publications.

Dozier Jr, R. W. (1992). *Codes of Evolution*. New York: Crown.

Eyler, J., Giles, D. E., & Schmeide, A. (1996). *A Practitioner's Guide to Reflection in Service-learning: Student Voices & Reflections*. Nashville, TN: Vanderbilt University.

Freire, P. (1970). *Pedagogy of the Oppressed*. New York: Continuum.

Gass, M. A. (1993). *Adventure Therapy*. Dubuque, IA: Kendall-Hunt.

Gladwell, M. (2007). *Blink: The Power of Thinking without Thinking*. New York: Back Bay Books.

Harrison, R. S., & Short, R. R. (2001). *Waterline Model of Diagnostic and Therapeutic Intervention*. Kenmore, WA: Leadership Institute of Seattle.

Jensen, E. (2000). *Brain-based Learning & Teaching*. San Diego, CA: The Brain Store.

Johnson, D. W., Johnson, R. T., Smith, K. A., & Center, C. L. (1989). *Cooperative Learning*. Edina, MN: Interaction Book Company.

Knapp, C. E. (1992). *Lasting Lessons: A Teacher's Guide to Reflecting on Experience*. Charleston, WV: ERIC.

Luckner, J. L., & Nadler, R. S. (1997). *Processing the Experience: Strategies to Enhance and Generalize Learning*. Dubuque, IA: Kendall-Hunt.

Napier, R., & Gershenfeld, M. K. (1993). *Groups: Theory and Practice*. Boston, MA: Houghton Mifflin.

Noddings, N. (2005). *The Challenge to Care in Schools: An Alternative Approach to Education*. New York: Teachers College Press.

Paul, R., & Binker, A. (1990). Socratic questioning. In R. Paul (Ed.), *Critical Thinking* (pp. 269–298). Rohnert Park, CA: Center for Critical Thinking and Moral Critique.

Pearson, M., & Smith, D. (1985). *Debriefing in Experience-based Learning*. London: Kogan Page.

Schon, D. A. (1983). *The Reflective Practitioner: How Professionals Think in Action*. New York: Basic Books.

Tuckman, B. W. (1965). Developmental sequence in small groups. *Psychological Bulletin, 63*(6), 384.

Vygotsky, L. S. (1978). *Mind and Society: The Development of Higher Mental Processes*. Boston, MA: Harvard University Press.

Yerkes, R. M., & Dodson, J. D. (1908). The relation of strength of stimulus to rapidity of habit formation. *Journal of Comparative Neurology and Psychology, 18*(5), 459–482.

Chapter 7

Assessment and Experiential Education

The most important method of education... always has consisted of that in which the pupil was urged to actual performance.

(Albert Einstein, 1954, p. 60)

INTRODUCTION

If your college campus is anything like mine, "assessment" is often considered the "a-word" among teaching faculty. Typically, there are three basic types of faculty reaction to the "a-word"—messianic fervor, various forms of agnosticism, and equally fervent denial. Those who "preach the assessment gospel" tend to have received the good news at a conference, a workshop, or some other context where assessment strategies were presented in a way that made sense—causing them to become enthusiastic about implementing various initiatives back on campus. Or they may be deans, department chairs, or other academic administrators who understand how critical assessment is becoming for things like accreditation and for demonstrating the return on investment of a college degree or particular program. Those in the middle, the agnostics, are not averse to the "a-word," but they tend to feel that assessment is time-consuming and somewhat confusing in terms of methodology. They also remain somewhat skeptical as to whether or not all this "bean counting" makes a real difference in student learning. The last group, the "deniers," adamantly reject the new assessment *sturm und drang*. They think that current forms of grading and evaluation have worked pretty well over the years and they see no reason to adopt all these fancy new rubrics and portfolios of learning. They tend to view assessment talk as top-down "administrivia" and something that distracts from real teaching and learning. Like almost everything in life, each of these perspectives holds some legitimacy. However, each group also misses the point in terms of the value of assessment in student learning.

Those who preach the gospel of assessment can sometimes rightfully be accused of conflating data and information with knowledge and wisdom. We can become so caught up in assessing everything that, in the end, we spend all our time collecting and precious little time using this assessment to impact student learning or institutional improvement. It is not that assessment itself is a bad idea. The more important question is—are we spending time assessing the most important things? In other words, is the "squeeze worth the juice?" And are we closing the loop with this data through specific adjustments and improvement? Those in the middle, the agnostics, often complain that there isn't enough time to do all this assessment and they wonder about its effectiveness. But this group, too, may be overlooking the *variety of forms* assessment can take and how assessment can be used meaningfully and effectively as part of the educational process rather than just an after-the-fact summation. Finally, the deniers consider the whole assessment discourse to be educationally bankrupt but this group ignores how much has changed in the context of teaching and learning with the rise of the Internet. As Bowen (2012) argues:

> Motivation . . . is related to relevance and traditional assessment fails on that score. When content was more rare and valuable, it was easier to see the straight line from good testing to success in life. Today, it is hard to argue that doing well on closed-book tests prepares you for anything except more testing: college remains one of the last places where the ability to take tests matters both to get in and to get out. We should either change our mode of assessment or find new ways to demonstrate its relevance.
>
> (pp. 182–183)

So where does the "truth" of assessment reside? We are after, I think, what Qualters (2010) argues is that sweet spot between meeting criteria for what is widely known as effective assessment and what seems "reasonable, doable, and logical to faculty"(p. 60). If I could wave my magic wand I would take away the term "assessment" on college campuses and replace it with a simple question: "How do we know what we are doing is working?" In the end, this is a question all of us (I hope) can agree is essential to answer. In this chapter, we will explore the landscape of assessment in the college context, with a particular focus on experiential education. We will begin with some operative definitions, and a discussion of some of the common problems and challenges in assessing experiential education. Then, we will explore some of the basic best practices in assessment regardless of what educational process you may be employing. Finally, we will move back to considering the assessment context of experiential education more specifically and discuss strategies and methods that can be initiated at various scales (classroom-level and program-level).

DEFINING ASSESSMENT

According to Walvoord (2009), "[a]ssessment of student learning is the systematic gathering of information about student learning and the factors that affect learning, undertaken with the resources, time, and expertise available, for the purposes of improving learning" (quoted in Qualters, 2010, p. 55). There are generally considered to be two major forms of assessment: formative and summative. Formative assessment "involves the use of assessments (usually administered in the context of the classroom) as sources of feedback to improve teaching and learning . . . [S]ummative assessment measures what students have learned at the end of some set of learning activities" (Bransford et al., 2000, p. 140). In the discussion that follows, we will differentiate between student and course-level assessment and program-level assessment (what might more properly be called "evaluation"). Teachers are likely most concerned about student and course-level formative and summative assessment of student learning (the kind described by Walvoord and Bransford above). College administrators and program directors are likely more concerned with program-level evaluation. While it is beyond the scope of this chapter to go into too much detail on program evaluation, we will touch on a few of the key aspects of evaluation that connect most directly to experiential education.

THE CHALLENGES OF ASSESSMENT AND EVALUATION IN EXPERIENTIAL EDUCATION

Assessment of experiential learning can be quite a challenge. Take the example of trying to assess the learning outcomes from an internship experience. Let's say you have designed an internship experience with specific learning goals in mind and outcomes you hope the experience achieves. Here is an example of learning outcomes from the internship program at a small, liberal arts school (Hope College) in Michigan:[1]

1. Apply academic knowledge in a professional setting.
2. Observe and begin to understand professional organization and culture.
3. Clarify ones calling through reflection on the internship experience.

133

4. Critically evaluate the internship experience as an exemplar for the field.

These are solid learning outcomes. They can also be a challenge to assess. Unlike traditional testing, there is no right or wrong answer that we can mark students on. And, while rubrics are certainly used in evaluating traditional essays and composition assignments, for example, the conventions of good writing are more generalizable and understood. But in the case of assessing a student internship experience using Hope College's goals, how do we go about measuring how the student demonstrated her "calling through reflection on the internship experience"? This gets at the issue of what Wiggins and McTighe (2005) describe as the "challenge of validity" when assessing for understanding as opposed to correctness.

> A focus on understanding makes the issue of validity challenging in any assessment . . . These are challenges that face us all . . . we typically pay too much attention to *correctness* (in part because scoring for correctness makes assessment so much easier and seemingly "objective"—machines can do it) and too little attention to the *degree* of understanding (in which someone has to make a valid judgment). So understanding easily falls through the cracks of typical testing and grading.
>
> (p. 183)

Community-based learning, project-based learning, integrative learning, active learning—many of the pedagogical approaches of experiential education are oriented around subjective learning goals as opposed to "correctness." Because of this, teachers can feel uncomfortable giving grades and students can react negatively to such a different style of assessment. Students might ask: "How can you grade me on my internship?" Faculty might ask: "How do I come up with evaluation criteria for the service learning assignment in my course?" I once had a student complete a course evaluation where she spent the better part of four paragraphs arguing that my assignments and grading were completely unfair because I did not include traditional tests, quizzes, or exams. So it is not just teaching faculty that have certain set mental models of what assessment should look like.

In addition to student-level or course-level assessment, program-level evaluation can also be a challenge. As Ewert and Sibthorp (2009) argue:

> While providing convincing evidence regarding the process and outcomes of effective experiential education programs is a necessary goal, it is often

a challenging undertaking given the diversity of variables such as participants, program designs, and individual program experiences. While many of these variables can be accounted for through adequate research designs, others remain largely uncontrollable, but still influential.

(p. 377)

These "confounding variables" make it very difficult for evaluators to isolate out and demonstrate the effectiveness of experiential programs. Was the higher retention rate of a certain cohort "caused" by their participation in an experiential first-year pilot program or was it just a case of selection bias? How do we measure the impact of an internship program on a school's ability to demonstrate postgraduate career success? These can be complex evaluation questions that make it difficult to isolate out cause-and-effect relationships.

Nonetheless and despite these challenges, it is critical that experiential educators pay attention to good assessment and program evaluation strategies. The desire to attribute outcomes to learning outside the classroom on college campuses continues to rise. According to a 2013 article in the *Chronicle of Higher Education*:

> The proliferation of learning outcomes beyond courses is an increasingly common phenomenon . . . Institutions of all sizes and types—from California State University at Fullerton in the West to New York University in the East—are applying learning outcomes to things like advising, student-affairs departments, and extracurricular activities. The idea is to increase opportunities for learning and to assess and improve them. At the very least, it gives the experiences a label.
>
> (Berrett, 2014)

Demonstrated, evidence-based, comprehensive assessment is now the norm. Rhodes and Finley (2013) write: "[i]n the push for campuses to produce truly sound evidence of student gains and skill acquisition, increased scrutiny has been placed upon measures of learning that meet certain expectations of validity and reliability" (p. 15). And because experiential approaches and out-of-the-classroom learning outcome assessment is relatively new, there is little to go on in terms of structures, systems, and institutional history with this type of evaluation. The good news is there has been some good, recent work on best practices in assessment and program evaluation that can be readily applied to experiential education. It is those best practices that we turn to now.

135

BEST PRACTICES IN EDUCATIONAL ASSESSMENT

It is beyond the scope of this work to cover the entire range of best practices in educational assessment. For our purposes here, we will highlight areas that have the strongest connection to the practice of experiential education. Bransford et al. in *How People Learn*, make the claim that "in addition to being learner centered and knowledge centered, effectively designed learning environments must also be assessment centered" (p. 139). As we discussed in Chapter 5 on designing experiential learning environments, a major part of educational design is designing with the end in mind. Making learning environments assessment centered means thinking about assessment *in the design process itself*, not while the activity is already underway or (worse) at the conclusion. This is what Wiggins and McTighe refer to as "thinking like an assessor."

> As the logic of backward design reminds us, we are obligated to consider the assessment evidence implied by the outcomes sought, rather than thinking about the assessment primarily as a means of generated grades. Given the goals, what performance evidence signifies that they have been met? . . . Given the understandings, what would show that the learner "got it"? . . . Think of students as juries think of the accused: innocent (of understanding, skill, and so on) until proven guilty by a preponderance of evidence that is more than circumstantial.
>
> (p. 148)

How can we "prove" students are "guilty" of learning beyond a reasonable doubt? To Wiggins and McTighe, three basic questions should be asked in designing for an assessment-centered learning environment:

1. What kinds of evidence do we need?
2. What specific characteristics in student responses, products, or performances should we examine?
3. Will the evidence unambiguously demonstrate learning (or lack thereof)?

Designing in this manner, with the end in mind, is now considered to be a basic best practice in educational assessment. But this does not mean that such practices are widely implemented in classrooms and courses. As Bransford et al. argue: "[a] challenge of implementing good assessment practices involves the need to challenge many teachers', parents', and students' models of what

TABLE 7.1 The instructional paradigm

When thinking like an assessor we ask:	When thinking like an activity designer (only) we ask:
Given the goals, what performance tasks must anchor and focus the instructional work?	What would be fun and interesting activities on this topic?
What would be sufficient and revealing evidence of understanding?	What projects might students wish to do on this topic?
Against what criteria will we appropriately consider work and assess levels of quality?	How will I give a grade (and justify it . . .)?
Am I clear on the reasons behind learner mistakes?	What tests should I give, based on the content I taught?
Did the assessments reveal and distinguish those who really understood from those who only seemed to?	How well did students do on the test?

effective learning looks like. Many assessments developed by teachers overly emphasize memory for procedures and facts" (p. 141). On the other hand, experiential educators are sometimes guilty of designing fun but marginally educationally effective activities that do not adequately match learning outcomes with the activities and do not assess them in any rigorous way. In any case, best practices in assessment point toward a very different way of designing courses and units. Wiggins and McTighe summarize the differences in assessment approaches as described in Table 7.1.

In my own experiences in higher education I have found myself more often than not guilty of spending too much time on the right side of this chart and not nearly enough time on the left. "Thinking like an assessor" is now something I try to work on from the very beginning of course and syllabus formation and I find that the more I work with it, the more natural it becomes in my educational designs.

THE ROLE OF FORMATIVE ASSESSMENT

In addition to design considerations, the role of formative assessment has come to the fore as an overlooked element of effective learning environments. For too long, summative assessments have served as the primary method of assessing student learning. But such an approach flies in the face of what we now know about the process of knowledge acquisition and learning. Bransford et al. state:

[s]tudies of adaptive expertise, learning, transfer, and early development show that feedback is extremely important . . . Students' thinking must be made visible (through discussions, papers, or tests), and feedback must be provided . . . Opportunities for feedback should occur continuously, but not intrusively, as part of instruction.

(p. 140)

In the entrepreneurial world, this is an everyday part of the culture and ethos. I once had an entrepreneur tell me, "in my world, we *want* to fail. Failing fast is our number one goal. It is the only way we can move forward. In your world (higher education), you fear failure and seem to do every thing you can to avoid it." It struck me when I heard this that, as institutions of higher *learning*, we do a remarkably poor job understanding and working with the role of failure and feedback in the learning process.

This is where the idea of formative assessment comes in. Formative assessment involves continuous and on-going feedback during the learning process. And, as Bransford et al. argue, "the addition of opportunities for formative assessment increases students' learning and transfer, and they learn to value opportunities to revise . . . Opportunities to work collaboratively in groups can also increase the quality of the feedback available to students" (p. 141). Learning in almost any context you can imagine is simply much more effective when we receive feedback *throughout* the process, not just at the end. Additionally, students find learning more engaging and integrated if the feedback is tied to future activity. Fink (2003) calls this approach "forward-looking assessment" and states:

Forward-looking assessment incorporates exercises, questions, and/or problems that create real-life context for a given issue, problem, or decision to be addressed. To construct this kind of a question or problem, the teacher has to 'look forward,' beyond the time when the course is over, and ask: 'In what kind of situation do I expect students to need, or to be able to use this knowledge?' Then, create a question or problem that replicates this real-life context as closely as possible.

(p. 13)

An excellent example of this process is the recent interest in "gamification." Video-game designers understand the critical importance of feedback and forward-thinking assessment in user engagement. It functions as the very core "pedagogy," so to speak, of game design and structure. As Bowen (2012) states: "Games are really just an endless series of tests, a constant stream of problem solving and assessment. Future educators will need to understand how games take the part of school that most students dislike the most and make it fun" (p. 59). When we "gamify" the curriculum, we are essentially structuring in lots of iterative feedback while designing the learning for forward-looking assessment. As a player, you are exposed to a series of problems or challenges and you don't move through to the next level until you master them. And, more than just rote skill development, Gee (2003, 2005) points out that well-designed games teach important critical thinking skills such as systems thinking, sequential problem solving, and lateral thinking. The example of the UVA Bay Game introduced in Chapter 2 is an example of the power of formative assessment in gaming design and learner engagement. While immersed in the problem of creating a sustainable watershed for the Chesapeake Bay, students receive instantaneous feedback on their decisions and actions. This creates an almost seamless structure of on-going formative assessment and feedback that is difficult to replicate in the traditional student–teacher relationship. Educators will have to come to grips with the fact that there are *some* contexts where digital interfaces such as this simply offer better educational outcomes.

ASSESSMENT VARIETY

Finally, it is important to stress that an assessment-centered educational environment employs a variety of assessment strategies. There is no "one size fits all" or "grand unifying tactic" that one should use. The most effective form of assessment is to use varied strategies and make it continuous. Wiggins and McTighe refer to this as a "continuum of assessments" defined as:

> checks of understanding (such as oral questions, observations, dialogues); traditional quizzes, tests, and open-ended prompts; and performance tasks and projects. They vary in terms of scope (from simple to complex), time frame (from short to long-term), setting (from decontextualized to authentic contexts), and structure (from highly directive to unstructured) . . . [A]ssessment . . . should be thought of in terms of a collection of evidence over time instead of an "event". . .
>
> (p. 152)

Such an approach does not eschew traditional assessments such as quizzes, problem sets, and the like, but it does suggest that these must be placed in a wider context and plan for the demonstration of student understanding. At my institution, for example, there is a history professor notorious for her multiple-choice quizzes. They are very challenging and students always remark on this component of her classes. But she balances this with other forms of assessment. In fact, she considers herself a "critical pedagogue"—a school of educational philosophy (from Paulo Freire) that is often seen as oppositional to the usage of such tests. But she believes these quizzes invite more critical thinking in her students and hold their feet to the collective fire on class content. So long as there is a continuum of assessment, no single assessment method should be seen as antithetical to your objectives—regardless of what educational philosophy you espouse.

While there is much we can say about best practices in educational assessment, we have touched on several key elements that are most salient to experiential education. First, assessment must be thought of in the actual design itself. Such backward design thinking is critical to making sure the focus remains on learning for understanding and not either rote memorization or activity-for-activity sake. Second, we must understand the differences and distinctions between both formative and summative assessment. While summative assessment is more commonly employed in education, formative assessment methods are a critical component of learner-centered environments. Finally, within the role of formative assessment, varied forms of feedback and forward-thinking assessment strategies can be particularly effective and are most often overlooked in classrooms and courses. We will turn now to how a consideration of these best practices translates specifically to experiential practice in the college context.

ASSESSMENT AND EXPERIENTIAL EDUCATION

When considering what works with assessment in experiential education, we will need to differentiate between "activity and course-level" assessment and "program-level" evaluation. For example, a faculty member incorporates a place-based learning activity in her introductory Spanish class. As part of the course, she assigns students a specific neighborhood near the university to walk through and get to know.[2] She then assigns the groups a presentation (done in Spanish) toward the end of the semester that asks them to introduce the neighborhood to audience members (a public presentation) and share some reflections on their interactions. She evaluates the students on the assignment based in part on this final presentation. This would be considered activity-and/or course-level assessment. In another example, a college initiates a place-based pre-orientation program for first years that connects a required first-year seminar to purposeful engagements with the local community. Approximately 25 different seminars are participating in the pilot. This would be considered program-level evaluation. While both examples are incorporating the same experiential education methodology (community-based learning), they are doing it at different scales and require different forms of assessment and evaluation.

STUDENT AND COURSE-LEVEL ASSESSMENT

In considering course or activity-level assessment of experiential education, there are three key concepts to explore and consider:

1. Authentic learning products and performance.
2. Criteria and rubrics.
3. Learning portfolios.

Each is, in many ways, connected to the other. For example, one of the most important principles of experiential learning is the idea of "authenticity"— that is, connecting real world problems and scenarios to student learning. However, as we attempt to create such environments, we immediately run into a need to evaluate and assess this kind of learning outside of more traditional tests and quizzes. This is where rubrics and criteria come in. Yet the principle of holistic and integrated learning is also central to experiential education. In order to connect learning across multiple rubrics and criteria, learning portfolios are often used. While it is important to re-emphasize the idea of a "continuum of assessment" discussed above, these three areas, in particular, are most salient to our discussion and we will explore each in turn.

AUTHENTIC LEARNING PRODUCTS AND PERFORMANCE

As discussed above and throughout this book, authentic performance is central to experiential education. Dewey describes this value in *Democracy and Education* (1916):

> The most significant question which can be asked about any situation or experience proposed to induce [and reveal] learning is what quality of problem it involves . . . but it is indispensible to distinguish between genuine . . . or mock problems. The following questions may aid in making such a discrimination . . . does the question naturally suggest itself within some situation or personal experience? Or is it an aloof thing . . .? Is it the sort of trying that would arouse observation and engage experimentation out side of school? [Or, is it] made a problem for the pupil only because

141

he cannot get the required mark or be promoted or win the teacher's approval, unless he deals with it?

(p. 155, quoted in Wiggins and McTighe, 2005)

In terms of assessment, then, the key is to understand how to design and then assess authentic products and performances. What constitutes an authentic product? To Dewey, authenticity comes from the interaction between the subject and the object of study. It has to avoid a sense of being "contrived" and it has to have some measure of real consequence associated with it. To Wiggins and McTighe, an authentic task:

- Asks the student to "do" the subject. Instead of reciting, restating, or replicating through demonstration what he was taught or already knows . . . The student's efforts resemble or replicate work done by people in the field . . .
- Replicates key challenging situations in which adults are truly "tested" in the workplace, in civic life, and in personal life. Real challenges involve specific situations of "messiness" . . .
- Assesses the student's ability to efficiently and effectively use a repertoire of knowledge and skill to negotiate a complex and multistage task . . .
- Allows opportunities to rehearse, practice, consult resources, and get feedback on and refine performances and products.

(p. 154)

In experiential education, authentic problems are viewed as a central feature of increased student engagement. The task, then, is to design experiential contexts where understanding can be revealed through performance. Wesleyan College in Georgia, for example, redesigned their first year seminar series around the idea of design thinking from the Stanford Design School.[3] The learning sequence in design thinking can be represented by a cyclical process (empathize–define–ideate–prototype–test) (see Figure 7.1 below).

In their first-year seminar program, the faculty created opportunities for students to experience design thinking on a problem of their choosing on campus around the theme of sustainability and food issues. One student group, for example, decided to tackle the problem of messy, wasted, and leftover food in dormitory refrigerators. In the "empathy" component, they conducted interviews and needs analyses with the end-users—the folks who use the common kitchen and the housekeeping staff. This led to a definition of the problem and an ideation stage where they brainstormed possible responses and

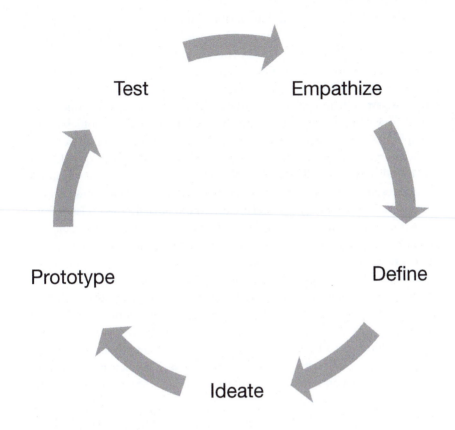

FIGURE 7.1 Design thinking

solutions to the problem. Then students worked in winnowing down ideas toward a single prototype. In the prototype phase, students actually built a prototype out of cardboard and materials. The point of the prototype is not necessarily to build something functional; rather, the process of building something tangible (even if symbolic) in a collaborative group creates a sense of concreteness and materiality that writing alone cannot replicate. The finished prototype then goes back to the user for "testing" and feedback. This, then, feeds back into the empathy loop all over again. A common phrase in design thinking is: "fall in love with your user, not your prototype." In the case of the messy kitchen, students worked on designing and implementing a new awareness campaign with a specific focus on the impact the kitchens had on the housekeeping staff.

The University of Oregon's Sustainable Cities Initiative (SCI) is another example of this kind of authentic performance learning structure. Each year, the program works directly with a city, county, or district and connects research needs and questions generated from the partner city's government agencies to existing courses and projects at the university. Students perform research in groups as part of their regular coursework in any given class. At the conclusion of their research projects, students present their findings to city officials. For example, for one Oregon city, geography students used GIS to research socioeconomic and environmental issues around public transportation ridership and overall city walkability. For another city, journalism students mapped cultural resources of Latino populations and made recommendations for how the city could better bridge cultural divides. Approximately 20–30 classes from across the curriculum and 400-plus students participate each year and the program is now being replicated at over 20 other colleges and universities across the country. The initiative has been described as one of higher education's "most successful and comprehensive service-learning programs."[4]

Both the first-year seminar at Wesleyan and the SCI program at Oregon serve as excellent examples of this concept of authentic learning and performance. As Wiggins and McTighe ask: "does the test amount to just simplified 'drill' out of context? Or does the assessment require students to really perform wisely with knowledge and skill, in a problematic context of real issues, needs, constraints, and opportunities?" (p. 155). In the case of the Wesleyan College first-year seminar, the design of the authentic task allowed students to wrestle with, and eventually demonstrate, the design thinking at the center of the learning outcomes for the first-year seminar. All of this project work was contextually situated within course readings, content, and topics around sustainability and food issues. Along the way, students also demonstrated and received feedback on the key writing, speaking, and research/analytical skills that were also central to the first-year seminar program. In the case of the SCI program at the University of Oregon, academic coursework in a variety of disciplines connects to real problems and projects generated by stakeholders outside the university campus, giving students the chance to experience a direct integration between theory and practice.

In this form of authentic learning assessment, the problem or task is clear but the ways of approaching it remain open and varied. The setting is "real"— it involves an audience or end-user of some kind, a set of collaborators, and messy work contexts (variables, outcomes, etc.). Solutions tend to avoid precise and pre-formulated right or wrong directions but are still a required part of the process. Evidence for success comes from the rationale and justifications of the proposed solutions. And, as one can imagine, this process looks a whole lot like what happens in the world outside of school. It also happens to be a whole lot more engaging both for students and faculty. In my own experience with authentic assessment, nothing motivates students more than knowing their work is both of interest (and will at least in part be judged) by someone other than me. In order to assess authentic products, however, one needs to understand the use and purposes of rubrics.

CRITERIA AND RUBRICS

Rubrics are often used in assessing experiential learning because of the likelihood that the learning outcomes are not right/wrong or yes/no in orientation—they are more likely understood along a continuum of understanding or competence. We can define a rubric as "a criterion-based scoring guide consisting of a fixed measurement scale . . . and descriptions of the characteristics for each score point" (Wiggins and McTighe, 2005, p. 173). In order to use rubrics, criteria have to be formulated that clearly specify what is to be assessed to determine whether a learning outcome has been demonstrated. For example, if you were designing a community-based research assignment for a course on public history, you might have one of your criteria specified as "research methods." To get more specific, you might describe the criteria this way: "*Research methods*: The final student project demonstrates aptitude with applied research methods in the field of 'public history' including interview skills and transcription skills, and an understanding of archival structure."

"Aptitude" in this case is not about a right or wrong answer but rather the degree to which the student demonstrates understanding of research methods through this particular experiential learning project. To further specify, you might break this learning goal down by making criteria out of each element of the research methods you are assessing: interview skills, transcription skills, and understanding of archival structure. From each of these criteria, then, a rubric can be generated. For example, under "interview skills," you might have a rubric along the following fixed scale: Not evident; Limited; Adequate; Capable; Proficient. In terms of a rubric for this area, you might list the following:

- **Not evident**: The research project shows little to no evidence of understanding in the basic standards and structure of interview methodology in public history research.
- **Limited**: There is evidence of some understanding but also missing, improper, or poorly structured elements and/or procedures.

145

- **Adequate**: There is evidence of understanding and all the basic elements are present and accurately demonstrated. Several areas need more consistent application or effort in application.
- **Capable**: There is strong evidence of understanding and it is consistently and coherently expressed in all the elements.
- **Proficient**: The research project demonstrates all the elements at an unusually effective level and serves as a model for the assignment.

More than just "busy work," creating effective criteria and rubrics can also actually help "frame" the experience as we discussed in Chapter 5 and give students an overt sense of the purpose behind the activity. As Bowen (2012) notes:

> When a rubric is made part of the instructions for an assignment, it provides a guide to the student. A good rubric should show your students both your criteria and your standards, and putting them into a table ensures that you provide both. Note that with a detailed and specific rubric, the assignment is apparent almost without further instructions.
>
> (p. 163)

As Fink (2003) notes, teachers should think about ways to involve students in either self-assessment using your rubrics or perhaps even in establishing the criteria themselves. He describes the difference between what he calls "audit-ive assessment" and "educative assessment" where audit-ive involves only backward-looking assessment (what we have called summative) and traditional grading. "Educative assessment," to Fink, involves forward-thinking assessment, self-assessment by learners, the use of criteria and standards, and frequent feedback.

Once you have created such a holistic assessment structure, it still begs the question: "How can all this be put together in a coherent manner for the student and for the instructor (especially if I want to allow for multiple opportunities for feedback?)." This brings us to the final key element of experiential course-level assessment—learning portfolios.

LEARNING PORTFOLIOS

Once we leave the traditional territory of the essay and the written exam, and we begin to think about incorporating learning that is happening both inside and outside the classroom, the conversation inevitably leads to the portfolio. As Kahn notes (2014), print portfolios have been in existence for some time in education. She writes: "print portfolios were meant to cultivate habits of metacognition, reflective practice, and self-critique among students and, in some cases, to demonstrate student achievement of defined learning outcomes" (p. 4). With the rise of the Web, portfolios became "e-portfolios" as early adopters shifted from print media to digital platforms. The benefits provided by Web-based, digital technology were quickly apparent and, as Kahn points out, now, in 2015, "the word on e-portfolios is out in higher education" (p. 4) witnessed by a significant rise in usage at all levels.

But what is an "e-portfolio"? It is, at its most basic, a purposeful, digitalized, collection of student work. While there is some on-going dialogue about distinguishing between different types of e-portfolios—assessment-based systems, demonstration or "showcase-based" systems, resume-based systems—the current technology appears to be moving to single platforms that can differentiate into all these various purposes. As Bass (2014) notes, e-portfolios are not so much about a "trendy tech tool" as they are about a pedagogical approach: "E-portfolios are at heart a set of *pedagogies and practices* that link learners to learning, curriculum to the cocurriculum, and courses and programs to institutional outcomes" (p. 35, emphasis in text). Because this set of pedagogies and practices is highly congruent with the pedagogies and practices of experiential education, it is no surprise that it is increasingly used in assessment of experiential learning outcomes. Kahn argues:

> In a larger sense, e-portfolios . . . embrace several ideas that have been central to the higher education innovation and reform movement that has taken shape over the past generation: a constructivist epistemology that puts students at the center of building knowledge and meaning, urging instructors off the podium and turning them into intellectual mentors and guides; high-impact practices that take students out of the classroom and into contexts that ask them to transfer and apply knowledge; and active, social pedagogies in which students create, integrate, and apply knowledge together.
>
> (p. 5)

This pedagogical description should sound quite familiar to readers at this point. Each of the characteristics described by Kahn above serve as fundamental approaches to experiential education. Well-designed e-portfolios work at all scales—at the level of the individual student, the course, the program, and the institution as a whole. They provide mechanisms for reflection, integration, and demonstration—disintegrating the learning silos that are so prominent in traditional academic structures. Proponents and practitioners of experiential learning would be wise to become very familiar with both the pedagogy and

147

the various platforms of e-portfolios. They will be central to the creation of both learner-centered and assessment-centered experiential learning in the future.

PROGRAM-LEVEL ASSESSMENT AND EVALUATION

As we discussed earlier, it is beyond the scope of this book to cover best practices in program evaluation in much detail here. However, because so much of experiential learning in higher education occurs at the program and institutional scale, it is worth pointing out several key facets of good program assessment and evaluation. Many of the best practices from student and course-level assessment apply with program evaluation. Ideally, we create new programs and institutional initiatives "with the end in mind." We think through the learning outcomes we hope to achieve and then purposefully design initiatives and summon institutional resources with those outcomes in mind. The reality, though, in much of higher education administration is quite a bit different. New programs and initiatives pop up all the time—whether as the pet-project of a dean, vice-president, or president, or through the generosity of a well-meaning donor. Program directors often find themselves awash in program implementation questions long before they can take a step back and think about assessment and evaluation. Then, when we finally do get around to program evaluation, we get bombarded with options—do we use NSEE (National Survey of Student Engagement) data? HEDS (Higher Education Data Sharing) surveys? Conduct our own surveys and program research? Attempt to correlate outcomes with graduation rates? With retention statistics? All of this can lead to a whole lot of what Botkin and Davis (1994) call "data" and "information" but precious little "knowledge" and "wisdom." Qualters (2010) suggests that program directors ask four "essential questions" when considering assessment of experiential education: "WHY are we doing assessment? WHAT are we assessing? HOW do we want to assess in the broadest terms; and HOW will the results be used?" (p. 57). This methodology can help administrators to stay focused on the "juice that is worth the squeeze" in program-level assessment and evaluation.

One other useful tool for program evaluation is the Logic Model. Logic, or sometimes referred to as "Outcome" models, are used in program design and evaluation in many social and policy sectors, but are only now just catching on in higher education. Finley (2013) notes:

> A logic model is a personalized institutional assessment map that allows all
> stakeholders to gain greater insight into the resources, processes, and range

of outcomes needed to engage campus constituencies more widely in assessment efforts . . . The use of logic models is a strategy for facilitating dialog and disseminating data to maximize inclusion in the assessment process. The model itself is not unique—it exists mostly in the worlds of government and grant agencies—but its value is as yet under-appreciated for mapping coherent and integrated assessment across institutions toward desired outcomes.

The basic premise of the logic model is the same as for the other forms of assessment we have been discussing—begin with desired outcomes and work backward. The benefit of the logic model design is that it is organized at the program and institutional level in terms of its categories—making it easier to implement at larger scales than the assessment strategies we have been discussing at the course level.

Logic models typically involve four categories: inputs, activities, outputs, and outcomes. The model is most often represented visually by a series of boxes read left to right like this:

FIGURE 7.2 Logic model design

Inputs are the resources brought to bear on the program or initiative—these can be financial, human, and structural (such as buildings, etc.). Activities represent the key activities or events created out of those resources. For example, an internship program could represent an activity. The internship coordinator, the e-portfolio system, and the financial support for students participating on internships would all comprise various resources or "inputs" to support that activity. Outputs are the measurable result of the activity. Returning to our internship program example, outputs might include the number of internships created as well as the learning exhibited by the student. Finally, the outcomes are the desired changes or results from the program or activity. Typically, it is encouraged in logic model development to begin the work "right to left"—starting with your desired outcomes, moving to what evidence would count, and then to activity design and finally resource allocation.

The benefit of logic models in experiential education program evaluation and assessment is its ability to resist the "activity for activities sake" trap of much program-level work in higher education. The key question to ask when we consider whether to initiate this new experiential venture or activity must be: "How does this help us achieve our student learning outcomes?" Too often such questions are obscured by other well-meaning but off-target objectives. In my own institution, our Career Education area, for example, ran themselves ragged several years ago offering lots of open workshops for students on "finding an internship," "preparing for graduate school," "dressing for success," and the like. Attendance at such events was spotty and the effort it took to arrange speakers, advertise, pay for pizza, and deal with all the assorted logistics was substantial. But, in the end, after all the activity, it was less clear how these events were actually helping us achieve our stated learning outcomes related to career education at Earlham. Now, after going through the logic model process, the career team is much clearer about where they need to be targeting their "inputs" and how to go about assessing the outputs to ensure we are meeting our stated learning objectives. A significant learning that came out of all this for us was a simple rule: no "open/general" workshops unless they were partnered with an academic department or other campus group. This one change has dramatically increased both the attendance and effectiveness of career events on campus.

CONCLUSION

As experiential education on college campuses continues to rise alongside a real need to figure out how to assess the associated learning outcomes, teaching faculty, administrators, and program-level directors must wrestle with the difficulties of assessing out-of-the-classroom learning in real and meaningful ways. The anecdote, the cherry-picked "star student" or class experience, and the passionate advocacy of the converted are no longer enough in this brave new world. The new assessment frontier reminds me of something I once learned in a wilderness emergency medicine course: "care not documented is care not given." In the same vein, we are moving into a place, in higher education, where "learning not documented is learning that didn't happen." This is difficult for those of us who wince at the idea of having to translate transformative learning experiences into rubrics, portfolios, and logic models. But, in the greatest Deweyian spirit, it need not be an either/or relationship. A pragmatic approach to assessment in experiential education is one where knowledge is situated within a framework for action (Biesta and Burbules, 2003). In other words, we have to be constantly mindful that assessment is really about individual, programmatic, and institutional improvement. If our efforts are not directly leading to change at one of those levels, we are missing the point and getting lost in the proverbial "weeds" of documentation and bureaucracy. We are, after all, not after complexity and complication but validity and usability. This is critical work for experiential educators and should not be ignored. As Qualters notes: "With a clear consideration of design that goes beyond perceptions into documenting learning, by developing new tools to capture praxis . . . experiential educators can move from the periphery of learning to demonstrating that learning beyond the classroom is a central component in higher education" (p. 61).

NOTES

1. Retrieved January 24, 2015, from: www.hope.edu/academic/intern/Learning%20outcomes.pdf
2. There was an actual experiential project, the "Barrios of Richmond," designed by Professor Chris Swafford at Earlham College and funded through an Experiential Learning Fund (ELF) grant from the Center for Integrated Learning.
3. See: http://dschool.stanford.edu/use-our-methods/ for more on design thinking. See: www.wesleyancollege.edu/academics/wise.cfm for more on the WISe program at Wesleyan College.
4. Retrieved June 18, 2014 from: http://sci.uoregon.edu/sustainable-city-year-program

REFERENCES

Bass, R. (2014). The next whole thing in higher education. *Peer Review, 16*(1), 35–36.

Berrett, D. (2014). Now everything has a learning outcome. Retrieved January 24, 2015, from: http://chronicle.com/article/Now-Everything-Has-a-Learning/149897/.

Biesta, G., & Burbules, N. C. (2003). *Pragmatism and Educational Research.* Lanham, MD: Rowman & Littlefield.

Botkin, J., & Davis, S. (1994). *The Monster under the Bed.* New York: Touchstone.

Bowen, J. A. (2012). *Teaching Naked: How Moving Technology out of your College Classroom will Improve Student Learning.* San Francisco, CA: Jossey-Bass.

Bransford, J., Brown, A., & Cocking, R. (2000). *How People Learn: Brain, Mind, Experience, and School.* Washington, DC: National Academies Press.

Dewey, J. (1916). *Education and Democracy.* New York: Macmillan.

Einstein, A. (1954). *Ideas and Opinions.* New York: Three Rivers Press.

Ewert, A., & Sibthorp, J. (2009). Creating outcomes through experiential education: The challenge of confounding variables. *Journal of Experiential Education, 31*(3), 376–389.

Fink, L. D. (2003). A self-directed guide to designing courses for significant learning. Retrieved January 24, 2015, from: www.bu.edu/sph/files/2011/06/self directed1.pdf

Finley, A. (2013). Logic models for learning-centered assessment. Retrieved January 25, 2015, from: http://leap.aacu.org/toolkit/learning-outcomes-assessment/ outcomes-assessment-instruments-and-tools/2011/logic-models-for-assessment

Gee, J. P. (2003). *What Video Games Have to Teach us About Learning and Literacy*. New York: Palgrave Macmillan.

Gee, J. P. (2005). Good video games and good learning. *Phi Kappa Phi Forum, 85*(2), 33.

Kahn, S. (2014). E-portfolios: A look at where we've been, where we are now, and where we're (possibly) going. *Peer Review, 16*(1), 4–7.

Qualters, D. M. (2000). Bringing the outside in: Assessing experiential education. *New Directions for Teaching and Learning, 2010*(124), 55–62.

Rhodes, T. L., & Finley, A. P. (2013). *Using the VALUE Rubrics for Improvement of Learning and Authentic Assessment*. Washington, DC: Association of American Colleges and Universities.

Walvoord, B. (2009). Reflection on assessment in departments and general education: How to be more realistic, effective, and time-efficient. Proceedings from New Association of Schools and Colleges (NEASC) Annual Meeting, Boston, MA.

Wiggins, G. P., & McTighe, J. (2005). *Understanding by Design*. Alexandria, VA: Association for Supervision and Curriculum Development.

Chapter 8

The Integrated, Experiential Campus

Most faculty spend a lot of time thinking about content and what to cover, but content delivery is not the core strength of a university, just as it is not for newspapers. The core strength of a university is integration.

(Jose Bowen, 2012, p. 285)

INTRODUCTION

As we move toward the end of our exploration of experiential education in the college context, a clear challenge remains—assuming we agree at this point that experiential education is an increasingly vital component of the 21st-century learning environment on college and university campuses, how do we ensure its implementation? As we have noted, curricular and pedagogical change of the kind expressed in this book does not come easily. The challenge of experiential education to longstanding educational structures means that integrating these approaches into the fabric of campus will take concentrated and sustained attention from faculty advocates and academic administrators. And this is critical work for those of us who believe in the educational power of the traditional bricks and mortar campus. As Bowen notes in the quotation that begins this chapter, content delivery is *not* the strength of the 21st-century university, but meaningful integration could be. Integration in this sense means looking at the totality of a student's experience—her coursework, her co-curricular experiences, her internship and research experiences, her study abroad experiences—and curating those experiences into a meaningful education through close student-faculty interaction. It is my belief that the pedagogical core at the center of this work is experiential education. But to do this and do it well requires a game plan. In what follows, we will first take a brief look at the evolution of experiential education on college and university campuses by identifying three "waves" of implementation. Then, we will examine the best practices for moving a campus into "third-wave" experiential education, where it becomes deep, pervasive, and integrated across curricular and administrative structures.

WAVES OF EXPERIENTIAL EDUCATION ON COLLEGE CAMPUSES

In considering how to implement experiential education systems-wide on college and university campuses, it is first important to see such work along a historical continuum. Various institutions are at different points along this continuum—some "early adopters" such as some of the colleges and universities mentioned in this book have been at this work for some time, and are benefiting from that sustained attention by realizing a robust and integrated approach to experiential education. This leading-edge status appears to have emerged from the ethos of the college itself (such as Northeastern University's co-op model), from faculty innovation in response to existential threat (in the case of Worcester Polytechnic Institute), or from charismatic academic leadership in seeing an opportunity for differentiation (as in University of Canterbury's response following the 2011 earthquake). Most everyone else, though, is short of this rather lofty goal. In looking across at the various experiential initiatives in higher education, I see three distinct "waves" of experiential education implementation.

In "wave one," experiential education is isolated and separated. A campus may offer volunteer opportunities for students, perhaps some faculty project-based learning in the curriculum, and a decent career services area for example, but these initiatives are relatively small and disconnected from one another. Many college and university campuses have moved past this wave in the last 10–15 years. I should say that there is nothing inherently "wrong" with being an institution in wave one. As I described at the beginning of this book, experiential education is *one way* to express what an institution values in the teaching and learning enterprise—it is not the only way. Presidents, provosts, and academic officers have to make hard choices about where to put resources, especially in the current economic climate. Having reasonably good but isolated experiential education offerings is not indicative of poor overall quality but it does represent, I believe, a lost opportunity.

This brings us to "wave two" where experiential education is more coordinated and connected. Many college campuses are reorganizing existing administrative offices under a single unit focused on some form of experiential or integrated learning. Sometimes such moves can highlight the benefit of collaborative activity and work flow, potentially saving institutional resources by avoiding duplication of services. However, more often such moves come with additional investments in an attempt to leverage the area as a distinctive for the institution. Since 2008, there has been noticeable growth in such centers and institution-wide initiatives focused around experiential education (see the Appendix). Yet while such moves make sense, without careful thought in implementation, consolidations such as this can become more of a "tossed salad" of component pieces that do not successfully integrate rather than the more hoped for "melting pot." And this is the identifying feature of wave two schools—there is some coordination and connection but not enough integration—especially with the academic side of the house. Robust and active experiential learning centers can be effective and useful to an institution, but it is the rare campus that has successfully stitched this "co-curricular" activity effectively into the curriculum.

And this brings us finally to "wave three" where experiential education is integrated across many, if not all, aspects of the institution including (and most importantly) the academic curriculum. Wave three experiential education is deep, pervasive, and "unavoidable" for both students and faculty. It is aligned with an institution's mission and strategic planning initiatives. There are champions and advocates in senior academic leadership positions. There is a robust faculty development agenda alongside bottom-up faculty innovation and experimentation. Assessment and evaluation is "baked into the bread," and there is a seamless interaction between curricular and co-curricular initiatives. Needless to say, wave three is "aspirational" for nearly every college or university that I am aware of. But important work in this area is being done and we are beginning to see campuses that can rightfully tout their progress in this area. Most campuses nearing wave three are not implementing experiential education as its own named thing. More often, they are implementing some form of one of the four core methodologies discussed in Chapter 3 (integrated learning, project-based learning, active learning, or community-based learning). In what follows, we will identify some of the best practices and implementation suggestions for any campus looking to move along the continuum toward wave three.

DEEP, PERVASIVE, INTEGRATED: BEST PRACTICES IN CAMPUS-WIDE IMPLEMENTATION

When tackling the issue of institution-wide implementation of experiential education, it helps to chunk out the approach to make things seem a bit more

155

doable and pragmatic. In my experience as an academic administrator, there are three basic buckets when it comes to institutional change: "easier," "harder," and "hardest." The "easier" or low-hanging fruit approach often yields quick results, but the fact that it is relatively easy to do also probably means that it is more vulnerable to losing the gains over the long haul. The harder reform initiatives often take more time, require more collaboration, can be more expensive, and are more perilous politically, but the return on that investment often means deeper, more pervasive campus change. And finally, the "hardest" bucket is the Mount Everest of organizational change work—it seems so daunting, complex, or unmovable that you can hardly imagine first steps let alone standing on the summit.

Before we get into the buckets themselves, a brief comment about best practices in organizational change work is in order. In my visits on other campuses, I have often been asked how we can "get the faculty on board" with experiential education. My first response to this is to politely suggest that we empathize a bit more with our faculty. They have multiple and conflicting goals and expectations thrust upon them—research, teaching, and service, not to mention precious little time and an entire life going on outside work. Don't misread a lack of response as a lack of interest. Faculty are like anyone else— they have to see compelling reasons for participating. And simply handing them a readymade "solution" to a problem they may not even be aware of will yield a healthy dose of academic skepticism (and rightly so). Vaillancourt (2015), in a blog featured in the *Chronicle of Higher Education*, recalls a typical scenario when it comes to academic leadership and change:

> It felt like many such sessions I have attended before—yet another example of a well-intentioned leader making a rational decision that seemed completely irrational to those most affected by the change. In this case, the leader viewed the situation in the context of national trends and knew that his decision was in line with what other universities were doing. But here's the thing: Most of the people who would be affected by the change have not been following national trends and have been protected from the financial data that influenced the original recommendations. To them, this new organizational design was a solution that emerged without an obvious problem.

In experiential education, we always begin in the students' world—what they already know, where their concerns and interests are—this is a basic tenet of constructivism. How ironic is it, then, that when it comes to organizational change work in the academy, we so often skip this step with our faculty?

Vaillancourt goes on to describe six key questions academic administrators must answer in the process of implementing institution wide change:

1. **Why?** Why is this change necessary? What evidence do we have to indicate this change is important?
2. **How?** How will this change be implemented? Ask faculty for help in figuring out how to handle the challenge and how to structure the process.
3. **Who?** Who will help? Build out support from early adopters and allies.
4. **What?** What will this change entail? Be specific and minimize what might get left to the imagination—that is where fear and assumptions flourish.
5. **Where?** Where will the impacts be? Be honest and upfront about how this change will affect divisions, departments, and/or individuals.
6. **When?** When will the change happen? Be as specific as possible about timelines for implementation to give people a sense of the size and scope of the project.

Many attempts at organizational change and reform are doomed to failure before they begin due to a lack of communication and attention to process. In my experience, faculty are not simply "resistant to change"; they are rational individuals who need to understand the reasons for change and want to be part of both the problem identification stage and the solution stage. Leave them out of the process and you will get resistance—it is as simple as that.

Once you have effectively answered Vaillancourt's six "Ws," you have choices to make about where to move tactically. Easier initiatives typically use time or financial incentives to implement change. I had a dean joke with me once that he could get faculty to do just about anything for a $250/day stipend. This is mostly true. Time and money get people's attention as both are in relatively short supply in the academy. External grant monies can also be of real help here to accelerate program development. Regardless of the type or source of incentive, appealing to the imaginative capacities of your faculty early in the process is often the most effective way to get them interested. Create open spaces for them to collaborate, experiment, and play. For example, consider encouraging entrepreneurial thinking through "pedagogical incubators." At Earlham (where I work), the academic dean's office funded a round of pedagogical incubators around the subject of academic and residence life integrations in the first-year experience. The problem statement focused around how to increase academic engagement in the first year by connecting coursework with co-curricular experiences. Faculty were then invited to submit short concept proposals. A small committee (including an outside reviewer) examined the applications and selected the best proposals. Winning teams of faculty (and you had to apply as a team) received funding in the summer to plan the initiative as well as a budget for implementation. The incubators were intended as testing grounds and experiments to see what worked and what didn't. We did not expect all of them to succeed or turn directly into long-term programs. The point was to get information relatively quickly about what faculty could get excited about and what students could benefit from. We also created "Experiential Learning Fund" grants, affectionately known as the "ELF," to support faculty who wished to experiment with experiential learning in existing classes, courses, and majors. Two rounds of ELF planning and implementation grants are awarded per year from the office of the academic dean, supported administratively by our Center for Integrated Learning. The initiative allows the institution to see where the energy and enthusiasm for experimentation exists within the curriculum while also giving teaching faculty concrete incentives for participation.

Another successful model is to work through a purposefully designed faculty development program. Recent research (Sorcinelli, 2015) has indicated the most effective forms of faculty development are the development of small, faculty learning communities and workshop intensives (i.e. multiday immersion programs). The Piedmont and Ponderosa Projects at Emory University and the University of Northern Arizona are excellent examples of intentional faculty development programs focused on infusing more place-based, sustainability-focused innovation into the curriculum. The programs typically involve a multiday immersion into the pedagogical approaches and considerations of place-based, sustainability-oriented curricula for faculty from across the disciplines. Faculty learn together through a combination of discussions and experiential learning out in the community surrounding the university. Follow-up sessions incorporating syllabus workshops and reflections on progress are also built into the design. In terms of outcomes, Eisen and Barlett (2006) note:

> At Northern Arizona, the Ponderosa Project developed a strong record of helping participants change not only what they teach but how they teach, and, among Piedmont Project alumni, three-quarters of the participants reported significant changes in pedagogy—especially in terms of getting students outside more often. In addition, the many aspects of the physical

and natural place of Emory and Atlanta are mentioned repeatedly as a driver of change in teaching approach.

(p. 31)

Regardless of the structure and design of faculty development with experiential education, do not dismiss the importance of faculty actually doing and experiencing the kind of pedagogy you hope to foster. There is simply no substitute for immersion and this is likely one of the key reasons why learning communities and intensives have been shown to be the most effective forms of faculty development.

Another common tactic in the "easier" bucket is the formation of some form of center or institution-wide initiative. This can be tempting as it can be done (more or less) quickly and without a whole lot of faculty buy-in required. But therein lies the limitation. Institutions that have rapidly pulled together such structures have found that while faculty buy-in may not be necessary in the short run, it is unavoidably required in the long run if the initiative has any hope of real success and integration into the intellectual fabric of the college or university. I recall one story of an institution that created, by presidential decree, the "Center for Innovative Teaching." Faculty immediately and rather incredulously asked the question "Does the creation of this center assume we have not been teaching innovatively before?" And "Is the center the only place on campus, then, that knows about innovative teaching?" When administrative structures like this pop up overnight and without robust faculty consultation, they run the risk of bad first impressions like this with the faculty. Directors of such centers then have a lot of heavy lifting to do to repair the damage to faculty partnerships by such decisions and it is critical that experiential initiatives have significant ground-up support.

Moving from "easier" forms of implementation to "harder," we move from "carrot" kinds of incentives to "stick" incentives. While it is always preferable to have willing and enthusiastic participation freely offered from faculty, sometimes a little more prodding is required. Institutions have typically tried several tactics here, including revising teaching evaluation and tenure criteria. This, for obvious reasons, can be a long and difficult process depending on an institution's governance processes. But there can be spaces in between to generate incentives for change. For example, at Earlham, the academic dean requests an annual report from each teaching faculty member that accounts for courses taught, number of advisees, committee service, and scholarly activity. With little effort, we added an additional section to the report that asked faculty to report on "any incorporation of experiential, integrative, or community-based learning in your teaching or scholarship below." This serves two functions. First, it signals to the faculty that the academic dean cares enough about this sort of activity that he or she is asking about it. Second, it allows the institution to create an annual assessment and tracking system for this work among the faculty. Adding this to the annual report structure was relatively easy to do and served some of the same purposes as more significant (and difficult) changes to tenure criteria.

Another "in between" space revolves around what we can signal to pre-tenure faculty about the expectations around pedagogical experimentation and risk-taking. We often hear, from younger faculty, that they feel disincentivized to experiment in the classroom because they worry about the impact of such risk-taking on their student evaluations (and subsequent tenure review). A glance at most institutions' course evaluations reveals that they are not truly teaching evaluations—they are closer to "customer satisfaction surveys." Young faculty are rightly concerned that if their students are not "happy" with their class and their teaching approach, this will show up on the evaluation and, hence, in their tenure file. This creates a scenario whereby pre-tenure faculty can succumb to "playing it safe." How can we encourage more pedagogical risk-taking and experimentation? For one, the review process can specifically state that the institution is looking for evidence of pedagogical risk-taking and expects to see signs of failure (and subsequent learning) in the reflective self-evaluation. Second, the course evaluations themselves can be revised to ask students to be more reflectively rigorous on the teaching and learning that occurred in the class and focus less on whether they "liked" the course and the instructor or not. Another option is to take a renewed look at teaching load, and examine whether and how the current system encourages faculty to do more experiential and integrated work, or discourages it through how load is calculated. We cannot blame faculty for eschewing more time-consuming experiential pedagogy if they are not rewarded for it through an acknowledgment of load.

The final group of tactics to consider fall into the "hardest" bucket because they involve changing campus structures that are firmly entrenched—either physically (in the case of buildings, classrooms, and academic calendars) or symbolically (in the case of the course and credit-hour). As we have noted in other parts of this book, the typical college campus is fundamentally unchanged from the early beginnings of the university model in Europe. At one level, this is comforting, and gives us a sense of the timelessness and importance of educational traditions. However, at another level, it can significantly curtail pedagogical innovation. As David Orr (2002) has argued, our buildings teach too:

160

The design of buildings and landscape is thought to have little or nothing to do with the process of learning or the quality of scholarship that occurs in a particular place. But in fact, buildings and landscape reflect a hidden curriculum that powerfully influences the learning process.

(p. 128)

Fixed seating, stadium lecture halls, drab classrooms, and inattention to place can make it very difficult to foster experiential learning. Further, every resource poured into the physical plant of the campus is a possible resource pulled away from engagement and integration into the larger community. We have built our current college campus physical plants around the value of institutional self-reliance when we should be promoting community inter-dependence. Clearly, we won't be raising all our buildings and starting from scratch any time soon. But we should be asking hard questions every time a new construction project is envisioned in the campus master plan. How will this building facilitate active, experiential learning? How is it connected to the larger community? What will it "teach"?

In addition to our classrooms and buildings, the academic calendar repre-sents another firmly entrenched structure that can be very difficult to change. In almost every talk I have with faculty across the country, at some point the conversation turns toward the academic calendar. Without changes to the traditional semester system, it is very challenging to implement certain kinds of experiential education. As Blumenstyke notes:

what worked in the 19th century as a tool for educational innovation—rethinking the academic calendar—is even more relevant today . . . this low-tech approach to reinvention has become a crucial piece of [college] strategy. The approaches include semesters and summer terms with mini-sessions embedded within them

(p. B7)

While some colleges have moved to the "block plan" such as Colorado College where students take one course at a time, this most radical reorgan-ization is outside the bounds of what most colleges would consider. Here again, the "in between spaces" are where the feasible reform can be done. The last decade has witnessed a rise in the development of "May terms" and "J-terms" that have enabled more experiential immersive study, for example. Some schools have more purposefully incorporated their breaks into "time on" as opposed to "time off" by connecting classroom content with some form of experiential field study. The summer months also open up a whole host of potential experiential projects with students, provided the finance and load structures can be worked out. Another idea emerged recently in a conversation among faculty at a conference: what if we offered a "lightning semester," a four-day open space within the semester that would permit pedagogical play among students and faculty? Students could offer mini-courses, for example, alongside faculty-led courses, trips, and experiences. The point of all of this is that even within rather rigid academic calendar structures, with a little creativity and ingenuity, opportunities for more experiential education can be created.

A final, and perhaps most difficult institutional structure is the "academic currency" of higher education itself—the credit hour and the course. Increasingly, "seat time" as the designation for learning is being questioned. As Bowen (2012) notes:

> Units of university curricula are also historical holdovers: no research demonstrated that a 15-week semester with courses meeting three times a week was the best unit of learning . . . [O]nline education will challenge all of our packaging units, and now would be a good time to rethink some better ways to organize our product . . . There is no evidence that 50-minute lectures or discussions are optimized units of learning.
>
> (pp. 254–255)

Initiatives such as the Lumina Foundation's "Degree Qualifications Profile" have shifted the conversation from the credit hour and course-based teaching to a more competency- and proficiency-based, developmental approach to student learning. This kind of shift requires a paradigmatic change in the structure of the university. If the value of a degree is no longer in a collection of courses and credits aligned with passing grades, how do we organize ourselves and our work with students? For example, many institutions have a general education system that requires students take a certain set of courses from across the disciplines in addition to their major in order to graduate. Some schools have shifted from a divisional-based alignment to a "ways of knowing" approach organized thematically that cut across the disciplines. But what if we moved even further to a general education system designed around competencies and proficiencies? It would no longer be enough to have taken a course and received a passing grade; the student would have to be able to demonstrate the acquisition of knowledge, skills, or abilities that might cut across a student's curricular and co-curricular experiences. However, to move to that system, we would need to rethink how we "count" learning within the current education system. The move to e-portfolios, for example, is one example of this shift in direction. "Badges" and certifications focused on specific kinds of skill acquisition is another emerging trend in higher education. Taken to its logical extreme, competency-based education might cease being an "add-on" and could replace the course and the credit hour as the central currency of the degree. As Bowen (2012) argues: "If employers start not only valuing badges or other skill certifications but also even requiring them, the traditional degree could be in trouble" (p. 258).

CONCLUSION

Making experiential education deep, pervasive, and integrated on college and university campuses is no doubt a substantial challenge. Almost everything about the pedagogical approach runs counter to longstanding structures, mindsets, and systems in higher education. This can sometimes make the work overwhelming to the faculty member or administrator championing experiential education at the local level. But in a conversation I had with Marc Schlossberg, one of the founders of the Sustainable Cities Initiative at the University of Oregon, he said he lives by the mantra of "just get started" (2013, personal communication). One can feel paralyzed by all the changes that must take place in the academy for experiential education to truly be integrated across all sectors of an institution. However, that complexity should not stop us from "just getting started." Starting small and with relatively easy initiatives and changes is, in fact, what just about every campus that is now "known" for experiential education did at some point. Folks looked around, saw an opportunity, and built the ethos and the institutional change from there. One of the central tenets of the field of Appreciative Inquiry in organizational change theory is to discover what is working and make it bigger (Ricketts and Willis, 2001). Once small successes begin to occur, they can form the basis for expansion and replication. And you will have evidence to back up your claims instead of trying to convince skeptics in the abstract.

For those of us who work in college and university contexts that emphasize the value of the residential campus, integrating student experience is, as Bowen suggests, our most important work moving forward. Given the rising costs of higher education, and the increasing availability of inexpensive alternatives, if we cannot express and demonstrate the value-add of the live encounter, we are in serious trouble. I cannot justify an undergraduate experience with the current cost structures if that experience continues to be siloed into atomized academic units, large lecture-heavy classes, and disconnected co-curricular experiences and career planning. However, I believe I *can* justify a four-year comprehensive and holistic experience that integrates all the aspects of undergraduate life into a truly transformative education for the students in our care. This is where the live encounter can indeed truly flourish.

REFERENCES

Blumenstyke, G. (2013). Academic calendars enter a season of change. *Next: Chronicle of Higher Education,* pp. B7–B8.

Bowen, J. A. (2012). Teaching naked: How moving technology out of your college classroom will improve student learning. San Francisco, CA: Jossey-Bass.

Eisen, A., & Barlett, P. (2006). The Piedmont Project: Fostering faculty development toward sustainability. *The Journal of Environmental Education, 38*(1), 25–36.

Orr, D. W. (2002). *The Nature of Design: Ecology, Culture, and Human Intention.* Oxford: Oxford University Press.

Ricketts, M. W., & Willis, J. E. (2001). *Experience AI: A Practioner's [ie Practitioner's] Guide to Integrating Appreciative Inquiry with Experiential Learning.* Taos, NM: Taos Institute Publications.

Schlossberg, M. (2013). Personal communication.

Sorcinelli, M. D. (2015). Faculty success for student success: Strategic investment in faculty careers at liberal arts colleges. Proceedings from Association of American Colleges and Universities (AACU), Washington, DC.

Vaillancourt, A. (2015). We like change just fine. Retrieved February 11, 2015, from: https://chroniclevitae.com/news/899-we-like-change-just-fine

Afterword

EXPERIENTIAL EDUCATION IN THE LAND OF THE MOOCS

I believe experiential education and the live encounter between students and teachers can serve as a galvanizing conception of effective 21st-century learning in higher education—a conception that does not defensively pit online learning against face-to-face learning, and that sees the value in the physically situated campus without dismissing the new learning terrain that exists outside the school boundaries. Throughout this book, I have attempted to thread a line between what I perceive to be the false dichotomies between digital learning and in-person learning. I find little value in staking claims at the extremes of these views—that online learning represents the future or that in-person learning is inherently better. The recent MOOC craze appears to be dying down but, as I argued at the beginning of this book, it would be a mistake to dismiss that historical moment as irrelevant. While it appears to be true that MOOCs were overhyped both in the popular press and within the academy, we must not conflate them with the utilization of online, digital learning platforms. Course management software, e-portfolios, mobile devices, and other Internet-based systems are here to stay and appear to only increase in use and significance by the year. The new generation of students are increasingly (though not universally) "digital natives" and come to college campuses expecting to experience significant portions of their learning through digital platforms. And, as we have seen, experiential education can easily happen through digital platforms. Simulations, game-based learning, and e-portfolios, for example, all support experiential learning in significant ways. The point, for bricks-and-mortar campuses, is to figure out a hybrid model—one that differentiates and discovers the best of both worlds—where to invest in and encourage online learning and where to invest in and encourage in-person learning.

That said, it would be a mistake, I believe, to allow our digital platforms to "manage us," ceasing to be just a tool and becoming both the end and the means of educational process. Democracy, in my view, requires embodied interaction. While it is true that the Internet creates all kinds of online "communities," there remains a qualitative difference between those interactions and the physically situated kind. I am not sure that I want to live in a world (or educate students into a world) where they do not know how to be physically present with other people—to experience the feelings that come with working together, discussing across differences, and empathy. These are necessary components of a vibrant democracy. Just as we lament the loss of "neighborliness" with the advent of cable television whereby everyone retreats into their individual houses to worship at the alter of their flat-screens, we might also lament defining an educated person as someone who has learned everything they need to know from a computer.

Robert Putnam coined the term "bowling alone" (2001) whereby he discussed the fact that while the number of people bowling in the United States has increased in the last 20 years, the number of leagues associated with bowling has decreased. Putnam connects this to a decline in public, civic spaces in the United States and the growth in more individualized activities such as watching television and getting online. The pervasiveness of digital technology has created a similar trend, in my view, in education—"learning alone." It is incredibly easy today to learn something by yourself through online means. That should be celebrated, but among the celebration, we should not forget that all this learning is still "learning alone." And civic society requires more than learning alone. It requires relationships and a notion that our various strivings must, in the end, be collective and not just individualistic. Dewey (1916) argued:

> The devotion of democracy to education is a familiar fact. The superficial explanation is that government resting on popular suffrage cannot be successful unless those who elect and who obey their governors are educated . . . But there is a deeper explanation. A democracy is more than a form of government; it is primarily *a mode of associated living, of conjoint, communicated experience.*

> (p. 87, emphasis added)

This was one of Dewey's greatest contributions to our notion of democracy and democratic process—that it is not simply a form of government, but that it is a mode of living. Dewey recognized that for democracy to thrive as such, it must be practiced out and that schools were a vital public space where this could happen. As Martin Jay (2005) noted:

166

Beyond a mere political arrangement, democracy also has social and moral dimensions . . . to further this cause, Dewey argued, education for democracy was an absolute necessity. Such an education must be based on experiential rather than book learning, creative investigation rather than rote memory, and a transactional relationship between a child and environment rather than a passive, spectatorial one.

(p. 296)

If "learning alone" becomes the new normal for modern societies, it is difficult to imagine how that supports a vibrant sense of democracy as a mode of living. But perhaps we are too enamored with Dewey's "Vermont Town Meeting" model of democracy where everyone (mostly white men) sat in the same room and had a good old-fashioned discussion. Perhaps this new era requires new forms of deliberative democracy and digital platforms are our new town halls. But it is also true that while we claim we have more "friends" on Facebook, sociologists tell us we have fewer actual ones. And while we have unlimited opportunities to engage with diverse perspectives online, we increasingly read and listen only to those perspectives with which we already agree. "Learning alone" may be more efficient, it may be easier, and it is certainly cheaper in the short run. But the long-term costs for both the individual and society can be tremendous. As an increasing number of students choose "useful" and "easy" pathways toward degrees, liberal education becomes eclipsed by the market forces of individualism, return-on-investment, and workforce development. As Roth (2014) argues:

broadly based, self-critical and yet pragmatic education matters today more than ever, and . . . it matters far beyond the borders of any university campus. The demands for useful educational results have gotten louder, and threats to liberal education are indeed profound (from government regulators, from the business sector, from within the university). In an age of seismic technological change and instantaneous information dissemination, it is more crucial than ever that we not abandon the humanistic frameworks of education in favor of narrow, technical forms of teaching intended to give quick, utilitarian results.

(p. 10)

Like Roth, I believe that liberal education is not set against practical aims. There is a pragmatic sensibility (developed by Dewey and other scholars in the American Pragmatist tradition) that views experience and inquiry together in ways that enrich and inform both personal and civic life. The sense that

167

liberal education cannot also be useful or that experiential education cannot also be liberal is fundamentally misguided. We can and should leave such simplistic dichotomies behind. That being said, there are real threats to liberal education represented by these two extremes. Taken too far, a defense of the academy as a place for intellectual activity divorced from a robust sense of civic engagement creates an impoverished democracy. Richard Rorty (1998) noted:

> a contemporary American student may well emerge from college less convinced that her country has a future than when she entered. She may also be less inclined to think that political initiatives can create such a future. The *spirit of detached spectatorship*, and the inability to think of American citizenship as an opportunity for action, may already have entered such a student's soul.
>
> (p. 11, emphasis added)

At its worst, a defense of liberal education leads to an articulation of teaching and learning that promotes Rorty's "detached spectatorship." This speaks to the oft-repeated "ivory tower" critique of the university. We cannot graduate "spectators" engorged with theory but not enough practice, and we cannot continue to produce faculty scholarship too far removed from any sense of "public intellectualism." At the same time, an education overly focused on "usefulness" creates another kind of democratic threat. Here, we graduate spectators of a different kind—students who may be "employed" and/or "employable" but never fully capable of understanding their freedom. In *The Dialetic of Freedom*, Greene (1988) states:

> They allow themselves to become what Christopher Lasch called 'minimal selves' (1984, p. 59). . . In such circumstances, what difference does it make to see oneself as endowed with freedom or even with 'certain inalienable rights'? . . . Stunned by hollow formulas, media-fabricated sentiments, and cost benefit terminologies, young and old alike find it hard to shape authentic expressions of hopes and ideals . . . what does it mean to be a citizen of the free world? What does it mean to think forward into a future? To dream? To reach beyond?
>
> (p. 3)

So, if we don't want spectators in either sense, what *do* we want? Rorty describes democratic civic-hood as an "opportunity for action" (p. 11). This is the pragmatic ethos—one that places intellectual inquiry in transaction with the world beyond. Biesta and Burbules (2003) note that "Dewey's approach is different in that he deals with questions of knowledge and the acquisition of knowledge within the framework of a philosophy of *action*, in fact, a philosophy that takes action as its *most basic* category" (p. 9, emphasis in text). Knowledge-in-action provides a crucial liminal space, a threshold, between intellectual inquiry and notions of vocation and usefulness. Roth notes:"Access to a broad, self-critical and pragmatic education has been and remains essential for a culture that prizes innovation and an economy that depends on it. It also remains essential for a society that aspires to being democratic" (p. 3).

While such a defense of liberal education is important to express, it requires more than words on a page. Colleges and universities cannot simply retrench into defensive posturing about the value of liberal learning. The future of learning in higher education, particularly for bricks-and-mortar campuses, will consist of increasing pressures to effectively express the value proposition of the face-to-face residential experience in light of sustained competitive pressure from cheaper, online educational structures and narrowly utilitarian conceptualizations of education. To hold true to the broader civic aims inherent in the mission of higher education, then, there is new terrain to explore in Rorty and Dewey's pragmatic call for more knowledge-in-action. It is here that experiential education, properly conceived and implemented, offers significant promise.

What does this mean for the future of higher education? Bowen has a provocative vision:

> Like music, higher education will almost certainly move forward as competing live and recorded products. Like live music, live higher education can be an experience that remains unique, varied, social, and highly customized to individual audiences. On the other hand, online education is like recorded music: cheaper and more private but with higher expectations of quality. None of the new delivery systems for music killed live performance: the experiences are different, and they appeal to different people at different times.
>
> (pp. 231–232)

Experiential education facilitates the live encounter. Internships, off-campus study opportunities, service learning, project-based learning, and co-curricular residential experiences function like Bowen's "live performances." University and college campuses must create structures to enable more of this to happen more of the time. These sorts of live encounters cannot be "learned alone." They cannot be readily scaled and outsourced online—they only happen through careful and purposeful orchestration of social experience. And this, then, can be the value proposition of liberal learning on the residential campus. But at the moment, experiential education of this sort remains a more or less marginal player to the bulk of intellectual activity on the typical university campus. This is a very vulnerable place to be in given the current competitive climate. As online learning continues to improve in quality all while offering its product at a much lower price, it will have a very compelling competitive advantage over the traditional bricks-and-mortar educational approach. A new vision for the value proposition of liberal learning on the residential college campus—one that is explicitly civic-minded, public, social, and experiential, must emerge as a viable alternative to the private, individualized, and spectatorial offerings of the online universe.

The successful residential college of the future will specialize in curating transformative experiences for its students. The local community around the college will be utilized extensively as a site of learning through community-based learning and research. After all, the local community is something that cannot be replicated or generalized (it is "local" after all) and represents a huge potential asset to the college or university if leveraged appropriately. The successful residential campus of the future will differentiate various forms of educative experience—some "high touch" and others "high tech" to both bring down costs and maximize the value of the live encounter where it does happen. The successful residential university of the future will be able to create a seamless interaction between the co-curricular and curricular sides of the college. In fact, the terms themselves will dissolve as students see and experience learning in a variety of contexts. This will require new collaborations and partnerships between residence life staff and teaching faculty. As Bowen (2012) notes:

> If we can further integrate learning across campus life, we will have an ever more powerful product. We need, in other words, not simply more [experiential] teaching but also more coordinated approaches to creating encounters with faculty and reinforcing campus activities that link to our learning outcomes.
>
> (p. 287)

Finally, the successful residential college of the future will have teachers who both understand and can practice experiential learning pedagogy in a variety of forms. This requires a paradigmatic shift away from teaching content and toward facilitating student learning. As Palmer (2007) notes:

Like most professionals, I was taught to occupy space, not open it . . . A not-so-small voice within me insists that if I am not filling all the available space with my own knowledge, I am not earning my keep.

(p. 132)

The live encounter is not just for the student—it is for all of us on the 21st-century college and university campus—faculty, staff, and students alike. This is what experiential education can promise us—that if we remain open, that if we create the situations, structures, and systems for knowledge-in-action to happen, we have the potential to transform not only our students, but our institutions, our world, and ourselves.

REFERENCES

Biesta, G., & Burbules, N. C. (2003). *Pragmatism and Educational Research*. Lanham, MD: Rowman & Littlefield.

Bowen, J.A. (2012). *Teaching Naked: How Moving Technology out of your College Classroom will Improve Student Learning*. San Francisco, CA: Jossey-Bass.

Dewey, J. (1916). *Education and Democracy*. New York: Macmillan.

Greene, M. (1988). *The Dialectic of Freedom*. New York: Teachers College.

Jay, M. (2005). *Songs of Experience: Modern American and European Variations on a Universal Theme*. Berkeley, CA: University of California Press.

Palmer, P. J. (2007). *The Courage to Teach: Exploring the Inner Landscape of a Teacher's Life*. San Fransciso, CA: Jossey-Bass.

Putnam, R. D. (2001). *Bowling Alone: The Collapse and Revival of American Community*. New York: Simon & Schuster.

Rorty, R. (1998). *Achieving our Country: Leftist Thought in Twentieth-Century America*. Boston, MA: Harvard University Press.

Roth, M. (2014). *Beyond the University: Why Liberal Education Matters*. New Haven, CT: Yale University Press.

Appendix

Reference List of Experiential Projects and Programs

Below is a selected list of initiatives, projects, and institutions that connect directly to the kind of experiential work described in this book. This is by no means a comprehensive catalog and I am sure I have left out many programs and schools. The point here is simply to give the curious reader some concrete examples to explore.

INTEGRATED LEARNING

Northeastern University Cooperative Education: www.northeastern.edu/coop/

Augustana College CORE: www.augustana.edu/academics/core

University of Iowa GROW: http://vp.studentlife.uiowa.edu/initiatives/grow/

Mt Holyoke LYNK: www.mtholyoke.edu/lynk

COMMUNITY-BASED LEARNING

Oberlin College Oberlin Project: www.oberlinproject.org/

Siena College ACE (Academic Community Engagement): www.siena.edu/centers-institutes/ace/

University of Canterbury, New Zealand Community Engagement Hub: www.comsdev.canterbury.ac.nz/rss/news/?articleId=1625

Princeton University Community Based Learning Initiative: www.princeton.edu/cbli/

PROJECT-BASED LEARNING

University of Oregon Sustainable Cities Initiative: http://sci.uoregon.edu/

Worcester Polytechnic Institute Project Based Learning: www.wpi.edu/academics/ugradstudies/project-learning.html:

University of Delaware Problem Based learning: www.udel.edu/inst/

ACTIVE LEARNING

Brevard College: https://brevard.edu/academics/experiential-education

University of Virginia Chesapeake Bay Game: www.virginia.edu/baygame/

University of Minnesota Active Learning Classrooms: www1.umn.edu/ohr/teach learn/alc/index.html

OTHER CENTERS/PROGRAMS

Loyola University Center for Experiential Learning: www.luc.edu/experiential/

University of New Haven International and Experiential Learning: www.newhaven.edu/IEL/

Earlham College Center for Integrated Learning: www.earlham.edu/center-for-integrated-learning/

Index

175